WARBIRD**TECH**
S E R I E S

VOLUME 13

DOUGLAS
A-1 SKYRAIDER

BY KRIS HUGHES AND WALTER DRANEM

specialtypress
PUBLISHERS AND WHOLESALERS

Published by
Specialty Press Publishers and Wholesalers
11481 Kost Dam Road
North Branch, MN 55056
United States of America
(612) 583-3239

Distributed in the UK and Europe by
Airlife Publishing Ltd.
101 Longden Road
Shrewsbury
SY3 9EB
England

ISBN 0-933424-78-7

Designed by Greg Compton

Printed in the United States of America

TABLE OF CONTENTS

THE DOUGLAS A-1 SKYRAIDER

PREFACE

This book is the result of the combined efforts of a large and varied group of people. Being Air Force oriented, we were somewhat at a loss regarding the history of the Skyraider in Navy and Marine service, let alone the use of the A-1 by foreign nations. But a group of outstanding historians gave us their blessing and their help. Seems like everyone liked the old SPAD, and wanted to make sure the story of a propeller-driven aircraft operating in two different jet wars was told accurately.

Therefore, *special thanks* must go to our Navy-oriented friends, including Mr. Jim Sullivan and Mr. Dick Starinchak. These two gentlemen supplied a very large amount of Navy and Marine Corps photos, squadron information, and details found only on Navy and Marine ADs. Likewise, Mr. Walt Fink came to our aid with the loan of Navy flight manuals and information on Skyraider flight characteristics and Navy armament details. And Walt should know these things—he was a SPAD driver in the mid-1960s.

On the Air Force side, a great deal of help was provided by several individuals who worked on or beside the A-1s operating in Vietnam. Mr. Terry Love and Mr. Larry Sutherland provided many personal photos and color slides that were taken in-country between 1965 and 1968. David Menard, then a Staff Sergeant in the U.S. Air Force and an A-1 mechanic, reached deep into his personal slide collection of A-1Es, which he worked on during 1965 to '66 in Vietnam. His collection of early Air Force Farm Gate A-1 operations was crucial to the completion of the Air Force side of the A-1 story.

Mr. Larry Davis and Mr. Mick Roth delved into their considerable technical resources to provide the proper designations for the many systems and weapons used by the A-1s in both Korea and Vietnam. Mr. Larry "Mac" McMillen, a long-time friend, loaned a complete A-1E "Flight Manual" that provided many details not found anywhere else. (Air Force A-1s were a breed unto themselves!)

Our grateful thanks go to Mr. Bob Mikesh, ex of the Smithsonian Air & Space Museum, for his help in keeping the Vietnamese Air Force story accurate. And to all of the staff of the U.S. Air Force Museum for their continuing help. They are an incredible group of people, very knowledgeable, and most importantly, very willing to help.

To the dozens of others who sent photos, information, criticisms, and just plain support for this project— *thanks!*

Most of all, our heartfelt thanks go to all the air and ground crews aboard the aircraft carriers in the Yellow Sea and on the Korean airfields, as well as to the aircraft carrier crews (again) who performed almost flawlessly on Yankee and Dixie stations during the Vietnam War. Final thanks go to the Air Force crews who took a World War Two propeller-driver dive bomber and pitted it against the most sophisticated air defense system in air warfare history so "that others may live."

We salute you!

KRIS HUGHES AND WALTER DRANEM
1997

A VA-115 AD-6 Skyraider assigned to USS Kitty Hawk in 1961. The Douglas Skyraider, designed during World War Two, flew countless missions in America's next two wars in Korea and Vietnam, with all three services, the Navy, Marines and Air Force. (Jeff Ethell)

INTRODUCTION

It has been called many things over the years, some official, some not—and most names were not complimentary.

In the beginning it was the Dauntless II. Then it became the Skyraider. To the crews, the A-1 was known as the Able Dog, Spad, Guppy, Queen, Big Iron Bird, Flying Dump Truck, or simply the AD. The missions that the crews of the A-1 have flown run the entire military spectrum, from dive and torpedo bomber, to airborne early warning aircraft, to flying ambulance, to aerial tanker. The A-1 performed all of these missions with distinction.

Several A-1s during the Vietnam War even played the role of fighter aircraft with the air superiority mission. Victories scored over North Vietnamese MiG aircraft prove that they could fulfill even that mission—and in a jet war. The Douglas A-1 Skyraider has certainly proven itself to be one of the most versatile aircraft of the 20th Century.

As its original name implies, the A-1 has an ancestry that goes back all the way to the incomparable Douglas SBD Dauntless. The "Hero of Midway" was designed and developed in the pre-World War Two era, serving as both a scout and a dive bomber with the U.S. Navy and Marine Corps, beginning in 1940. But even at the height of its greatest achievements, the SBDs were made obsolete by newer designs, such as the Curtis SB2C Helldiver.

The SB2C could carry the same amount of ordnance, but it had a much greater range and flew almost 50 MPH faster than the "Slow But Deadly" SBD. Douglas needed an entirely new design to meet the new Navy requirements.

Douglas' answer to this dilemma was the XSB2D-1 scout and torpedo bomber. The new design was revolutionary in many ways, including the tricycle landing gear that replaced the tail-wheel designs common to all other Navy aircraft. The XSB2D-1 was also equipped with a pair of remote-control gun turrets, each mounting a pair of .50-caliber machine guns for defensive purposes.

Offensively, each wing had a single 20MM cannon. Ordnance could be carried internally in an enclosed weapons bay, or externally under the wings and fuselage. The maximum ordnance load was more than 4,200-pounds—a pair of 1,600-pound bombs internally, plus a pair of 500-pound bombs under its wings. For the torpedo bomber mission, the XSB2D-1 could also carry a pair of 2,100-pound Mk. 13 aerial torpedos on special pylons under its fuselage.

The XSB2D-1 had a mid-fuselage-mounted laminar flow, inverted gull wing, similar to the type seen on the renowned F4U Corsair, and it had it for the same reason—clearance. Power for the XSB2D-1 was to be the at that time new Wright R-3350, 18-cylinder air-cooled radial engine, the same

basic engine that was under development for the B-29. With the high-speed laminar flow wing and the 2,300 horsepower R-3350-14 engine, the XSB2D-1 was projected to have a top speed exceeding 325 MPH.

The prototype XSB2D-1 came off the Douglas Aircraft Co. assembly line at El Segundo, California, on March 17, 1943, and it flew its first flight on April 8. Flight tests revealed that the top speed was actually faster than 345 MPH, which was 20 MPH faster than projected and a whopping 64 MPH faster than the SB2C Helldiver.

Enthusiastically, the Navy Department awarded Douglas a contract to build 13 service test SB2D-1s, quickly revising the order to 345 SB2D production aircraft on August 31, 1943. That order, unfortunately, was short-lived. In early fall 1943, the Navy Bureau of Aeronautics (BuAer) revised the requirements for future dive and torpedo bombers.

According to BuAer, defensive armament was no longer needed due to the air superiority gains the Navy and Marine pilots had won during the war. Hellcats and Corsairs could handle any Japanese aircraft attempting to intercept the fleet and its strike forces. BuAer informed all the competing manufacturers that all new dive and torpedo designs should be developed around a single pilot with no rear gunners.

The Navy asked Douglas if it was feasible for them to modify the XSB2D-1 into a single-seat design to meet the new requirements. The Douglas engineers set about the task of converting the three-place XSB2D-1 to a single-seat aircraft with relative ease.

The dual cockpits were replaced with a single-seat design. Both defensive turrets and all the remote fire control systems were removed. A single sliding canopy was installed over a new streamlined rear fuselage fairing that covered the area of the gunner's cockpit. The large vertical fin fillet was extended through the area once occupied by the upper gun turret. The weight savings garnered by removal of the gun turret systems was eaten up by an increase in internal fuel tankage, which rose from 550 gallons to 640 gallons, bringing about a slight increase in range.

The rest of the basic design, including offensive armament, ordnance load, and the gull-wing, remained essentially the same. The designation was changed from XSB2D-1 (Experimental Scout Bomber, type 2, from Douglas) to BTD-1 (Bomber/Torpedo aircraft from Douglas), and nicknamed the Destroyer.

The first BTD-1 (Bu. No. 04960) came off the assembly line on February 15, 1944. In actuality, this first aircraft was the second SB2D-1 service test aircraft that had been modified to meet the new Navy specifications for a single-seat bomber.

On March 5, 1944, the BTD-1 took to the air for the first time. The BTD-1 was an impressively performing airplane, with a top speed of 345 MPH, a 1,650 feet per minute rate of climb, and a maximum range of 2,140 miles. Although it weighed almost 500 pounds more than the XSB2D-1, the performance of the two prototype aircraft was virtually the same. This performance wasn't impressive enough.

The competing aircraft (XBTC-1, XBTK-1, and XBTM-1) all had equal or greater performance, and they were already in the flight test stage. In July 1944, the Navy cancelled the BTD-1 contract. Douglas Aircraft Co. would soon be relegated to subcontract work on other manufacturers' aircraft designs if they didn't act fast.

The BTD-1 Destroyer was to be the follow-on aircraft to the SBD Dauntless. The BTD-1 had a tricycle landing gear, an internal weapons bay, and an inverted gull wing. First flying on March 5, 1944, the BTD-1 was cancelled in July 1944. (Douglas)

DAUNTLESS II

With the cancellation of the BTD-1 contract in July 1944, Douglas Aircraft Co. had lost a contract to build 623 aircraft. The Douglas engineering team of Chief Engineer Ed Heinemann, Chief Designer Leo Devlin, and Chief Aerodynamicist Gene Root had to come up with something quickly or the company would not have a major aircraft in the Navy inventory. Army Air Force contracts for the A-20 Havoc series and A-26 Invader would keep the company financially sound, but the pride having built the foremost dive bomber aircraft in Navy history, and now not building any Navy

contracts at all, moved the Douglas engineering team to new heights.

In early July 1944, following on the heels of the Navy cancellation of the BTD-1 contract, the Douglas team went back to their hotel room in Washington, D.C. Instead of bemoaning the Navy decision about the BTD-1, the team set down and began work on an all-new design. Heinemann, Devlin, and Root used all the latest information from manufacturers, plus wind tunnel results, aerodynamic and flight test results, and pilot reports from the combat arenas during the war. After working

through the night, the Douglas team made an appointment to meet with the same BuAer officials who had cancelled the BTD-1. Walking into the BuAer offices at the Pentagon, the Douglas team carried preliminary sketches and projected performance figures for an entirely new dive bomber design.

The Navy officers were so impressed with the overnight efforts that they offered Douglas a contract to build 15 of the new aircraft. The Navy actually just modified the existing remnants of the BTD-1 contract to cover the cost of the new design. The contract did

The XBT2D-1 Dauntless II was of the standard dive bomber configuration, i.e. external weapons carriage, straight wing, and a tail dragger design. It was just bigger! Rolled out resplendent in shiny natural metal, the XBT2D-1 made its first flight on March 18, 1945. The emblem on the cowling is the Douglas Aircraft Co. Test Division logo. (Department of Defense)

Production XBT2D-1 aircraft were delivered in the standard Navy Gloss Sea Blue paint scheme. The first unit to take delivery of the Dauntless II was VA-19A, the unit charged with service tests of the new airplane, at NAS Alameda. In February 1946, the aircraft was re-named Douglas Skyraider. (Jim Sullivan Collection)

One of the XBT2D-1 aircraft (BuAer 09109) was modified to carry an electronic countermeasures operator, with added windows, in its rear fuselage. Re-designated XBT2D-1Q, the aircraft also had additional AN/APA-69 ECM radomes on its rear fuselage. On production aircraft, the dive brakes were deleted to create room for the operator. (U.S. Navy)

have one new provision: The new aircraft had to be ready to compete against the other manufacturer's dive bomber designs in an upcoming competition, and the other manufacturers had up to six months head start!

The new aircraft was designated XBT2D-1. It was a straightforward design, with none of the radical developments that had highlighted the XSB2D-1/BTD-1 design. Gone was the inverted laminar flow gull-wing. The XBT2D-1 was a standard low wing monoplane with a straight wing. Gone too was the tricycle landing gear as the XBT2D-1 would be a standard tail dragger. These changes alone were enough to make the projected rollout date realistic to both the engineers and the production crews.

A Marine pilot from VMFT-10 taxis an XBT2D-1 assigned to the training squadron at MCAS El Toro, California, in 1949. Marine Skyraiders were identical to Navy aircraft, including carrying all Navy carrier launch and recovery equipment. (Jim Sullivan Collection)

On August 14, 1944, slightly over a month after the fateful Washington night session, the XBT2D-1 mockup was ready for inspection. It was quite large for a single-seat, single-engine aircraft. The XBT2D-1 was

The AD-1 made its first flight on November 5, 1946. The AD-1 was the first true production variant, differing from the XBT2D-1 only in the additional internal strengthening of its wing and the R-3350-24W engine. The designation changed to AD-1 in April 1946. (Douglas)

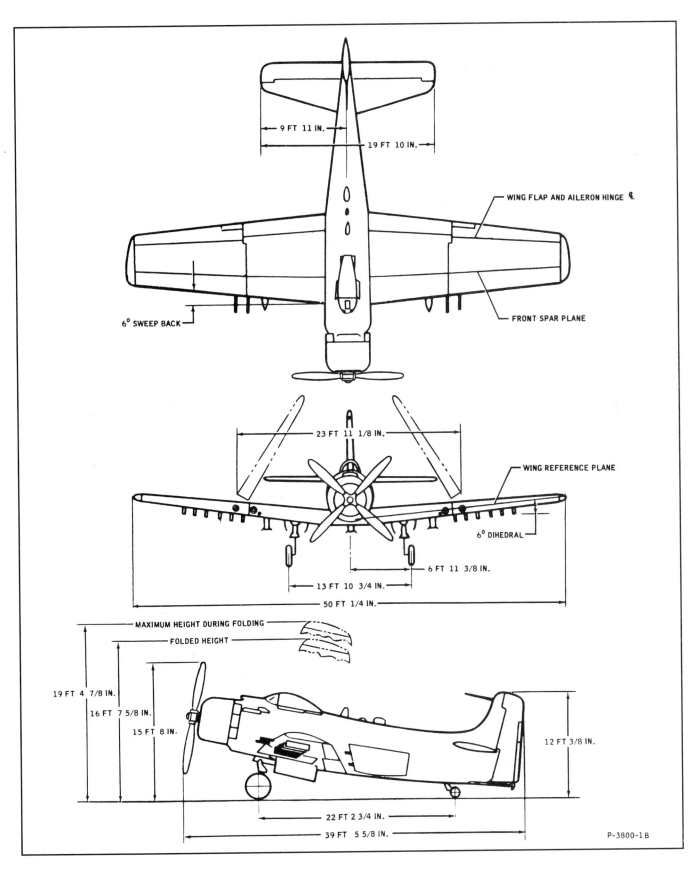

This three-view drawing of the basic AD (A-1) Skyraider single-seat variant clearly shows the immense size of the aircraft. All the AD variants had basically the same measurements with the exception of the multi-place AD-5 types. (Larry Davis)

over 50 feet in length, with a wingspan of almost 40 feet. Compare this to the SBD Dauntless at almost 32 feet long, with a 39-foot wingspan. As large as the XBT2D-1 was, it did not have an internal weapons bay that was called for in the Navy requirements. All ordnance would be carried externally under the large, straight taper wing and fuselage. Three large dive brake doors opened from the rear fuselage, one on each side and a third under the fuselage.

The wing itself was the proven NACA 2417 series maximum lift wing with a tapering section having 4.2 degrees of washout for low-speed handling. The wing root incidence was 4 degrees for better take-off characteristics. All the flying surfaces, such as flaps, ailerons, rudder, and elevators, were all-metal, which was actually lighter than previous fabric-covered units. The engine was the Wright R-3350 that had been intended for use on the XSB2D-1. The engine was mounted with a 4.5-degree downthrust, which minimized trim changes. The Navy Board of Inspectors put its stamp of approval on the XBT2D-1 mockup and work began immediately on the first prototype.

Eight months later, in mid-March 1945, the prototype was finished—some four months ahead of schedule. The Douglas engineers performed this feat by using available equipment off the shelf, rather than waiting for custom-built items designed specifically for the XBT2D-1. For instance, the rearward retracting landing gear

An AD-1 (09315) from VA-4B aboard USS Franklin D. Roosevelt, *carries the AN/APS-4 radar pod under its port wing. The tail code "F" and modex number "407" are repeated above and below the wings.* (Jim Sullivan Collection)

This VA-20A AD-1 (09199) has started to unfold its wings prior to a training flight from NAS Alameda in June 1947. The AN/APS-4 pod under its wing, was a search radar that could be used for both air and surface targets. VA-20A served aboard USS Boxer during this time. (Bob Lawson)

used on the prototype was borrowed from a Chance Vought F4U Corsair. Availability of the 2,300HP Wright R-3350-8 engine slated for the BTD-1 made it the engine of choice rather than wait for the 2,500HP R-3350-24W, which had been specified in the XBT2D-1's contract, to become available. Once again, the BuAer officials were so impressed with the Douglas teamwork and innovative creative skills that they increased the initial contract from 15 to 25 aircraft.

On March 18, 1945, LaVerne Brown, the chief Douglas test pilot, took the XBT2D-1 (Bu. No. 09085) into the air for the first time. It would be called the Dauntless II. The initial flight's test results revealed no great problems in any of the test categories. Indeed, the Navy test pilots at Patuxent River Navy Proving Ground rated the XBT2D-1 better than any other dive bomber design either in production or in the flight test stage. The biggest problem was a

An AD-1 (09204) from VA-20A flies over San Francisco Bay in June 1947 en route to USS Boxer, which is waiting at sea. The area immediately in front of the windscreen was painted flat black as an anti-glare measure. The AD-1 had only two 20MM cannons, with 200 rounds per gun. (William T. Larkins)

This AD-1 (09226) was assigned to VMAT-20, one of two Marine Corps training squadrons. The Marines began receiving AD-1s in early 1951. The aircraft carries a pair of Mk. 8 300-gallon drop tanks under its wings. (William J. Balogh)

An AD-2 (122330) assigned to the Naval Air Test Center at Patuxent River, Maryland, in September 1950, carries 12 5-inch HVAR rockets, two 500-pound bombs, and an Mk. 44 torpedo. The AD-2 was virtually identical to the AD-1 except for a strengthened, re-designed landing gear bay. (Jim Sullivan Collection)

recurring failure of the R-3350 engine, something that would plague other aircraft using the R-3350, such as the Boeing B-29. On May 5, 1945, three weeks after the first flight, the Navy awarded Douglas Aircraft Company with a contract to build 548 BT2D-1 Dauntless II aircraft.

That contract would be short-lived, though, as the end of World War Two brought many cuts in wartime programs, including the Dauntless II. The contract was first reduced to

This VA-155 AD-2 (122225), flown by Lieutenant Commander G.R. Stablein at NAS Alameda in September 1948, shows the AN/APS-4 radar pod under its port wing, near the enclosed main landing gear bay. (William T. Larkins)

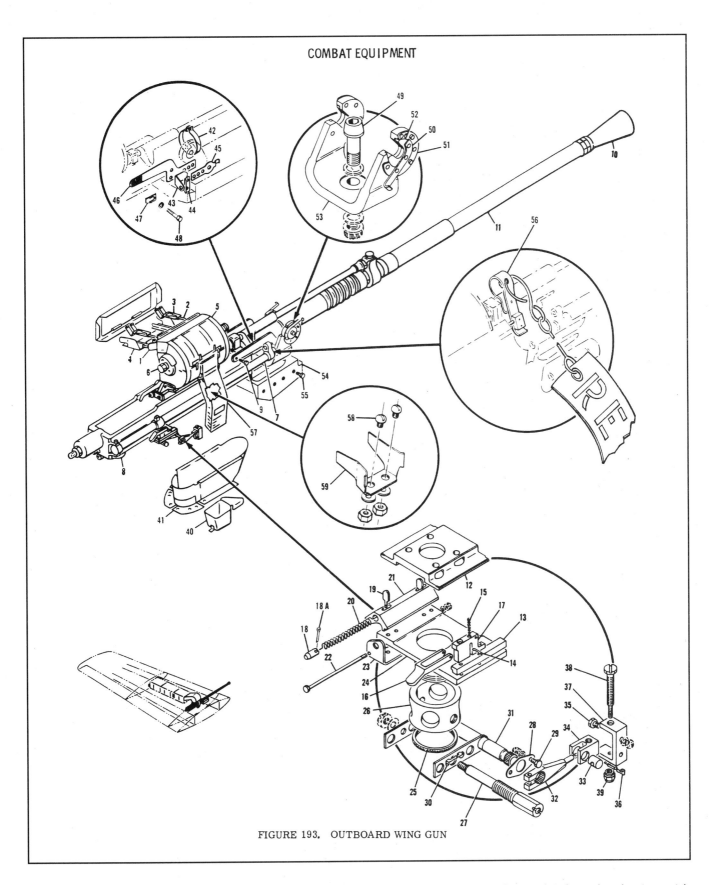

FIGURE 193. OUTBOARD WING GUN

The main armament for all AD Skyraiders were the M3 20MM cannon, one mounted in each inboard stub wing, with another M3 mounted in the outer wing from the AD-4 model onward. The M3 cannon had a muzzle velocity of 2,330 feet per second and fired 400 rounds per minute. The magazine held a total of 200 rounds. (USAFM)

A flight of Marine Corps AD-2s from VMA-121 flies over California in 1952. Based at MCAS El Toro in 1951, VMA-121 was the first combat operational Marine Skyraider squadron; it was deployed to Korea in October 1951. (Jim Sullivan Collection)

Aircraft B-411, an AD-2 from VA-194 aboard USS Valley Forge *in 1951, begins folding its wings after recovery from another mission against targets in Korea. The VA-194 AD-2 has at least 30 combat missions, which were recorded on the fuselage under its cockpit. (Jim Sullivan Collection)*

377 aircraft, then reduced again to 277 BT2D-1s by the end of 1945. In February 1946, the aircraft's name was officially changed to Skyraider. And in April 1946, BuAer revamped the entire aircraft designation system. All dive and torpedo bomber aircraft were redesignated attack aircraft. And the Skyraider was the first new aircraft to have the revised designation. Thus the BT2D-1 became Attack aircraft built by Douglas, type One—or AD-1.

The first 25 aircraft off the El Segundo, California, Douglas assembly line kept the XBT2D-1 (Bu. No. 09085-09109) designa-

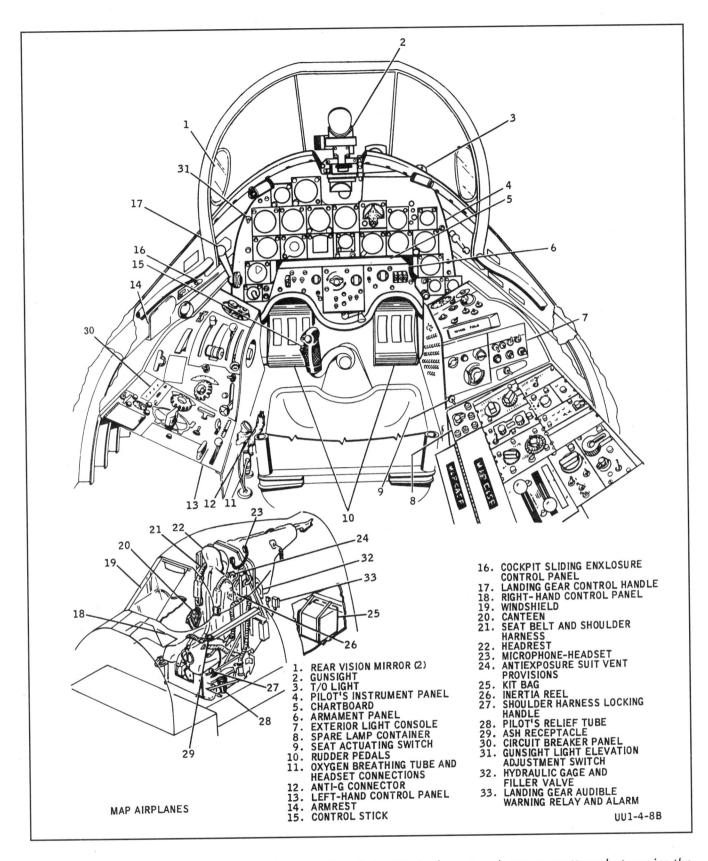

MAP AIRPLANES

1. REAR VISION MIRROR (2)
2. GUNSIGHT
3. T/O LIGHT
4. PILOT'S INSTRUMENT PANEL
5. CHARTBOARD
6. ARMAMENT PANEL
7. EXTERIOR LIGHT CONSOLE
8. SPARE LAMP CONTAINER
9. SEAT ACTUATING SWITCH
10. RUDDER PEDALS
11. OXYGEN BREATHING TUBE AND
    HEADSET CONNECTIONS
12. ANTI-G CONNECTOR
13. LEFT-HAND CONTROL PANEL
14. ARMREST
15. CONTROL STICK

16. COCKPIT SLIDING ENXLOSURE
    CONTROL PANEL
17. LANDING GEAR CONTROL HANDLE
18. RIGHT-HAND CONTROL PANEL
19. WINDSHIELD
20. CANTEEN
21. SEAT BELT AND SHOULDER
    HARNESS
22. HEADREST
23. MICROPHONE-HEADSET
24. ANTIEXPOSURE SUIT VENT
    PROVISIONS
25. KIT BAG
26. INERTIA REEL
27. SHOULDER HARNESS LOCKING
    HANDLE
28. PILOT'S RELIEF TUBE
29. ASH RECEPTACLE
30. CIRCUIT BREAKER PANEL
31. GUNSIGHT LIGHT ELEVATION
    ADJUSTMENT SWITCH
32. HYDRAULIC GAGE AND
    FILLER VALVE
33. LANDING GEAR AUDIBLE
    WARNING RELAY AND ALARM

UU1-4-8B

The cockpit arrangement was basically the same for all the AD single-seat variants, no matter what service the aircraft was assigned. The left console held the engine controls, while the right console held radio and other electrical system controls. The major difference was the installation of a radar scope in the upper right portion of the instrument panel. (Larry Davis)

Shook II, an AD-2 from VA-702, carries a pair of M65 1,000-pound bombs under its wings bound for the Changjin River bridges near Hungnam, North Korea. VA-702, which was an activated Reserve squadron from NAF Dallas aboard USS Boxer in April 1951, was called up for duty in Korea during July 1950. (U.S. Navy)

tion. These were the service test aircraft, except for minor differences, the service test aircraft were identical to the final production AD-1s. All but the first four XBT2D-1s were powered by the R-3350-24W engine as called for in the contract. The XBT2D-1 had a single-stage, two-speed supercharger, turning a 13 foot 6 inch Aeroproducts A 642-G804/M20A2-162 hydraulically actuated, variable-pitch, constant-speed aluminum propeller. The XBT2D-1 was 50 feet, 1/4 inch in length, had a 39 foot, 5 inch wingspan, and was 15 feet 7 1/2 inches in height. The empty weight was 10,093 pounds, while the maximum weight stood at 17,500 pounds. Maximum speed was 375MPH, with a rate of climb of 3,680 feet per minute. The service ceiling was higher than 26,000 feet.

The internal fuel capacity was a single tank that held 350 gallons, with a 150-gallon Mk. 12 external

This VMA-121 AD-2 carries a maximum load of three 500-pound M64 bombs, plus twelve 250-pound M57 bombs. Based at K-6, Pyongtaek, Marine ADs were used almost exclusively to support the Marine ground troops on the MLR. (H. Heiner)

A flight of Air Group 15 AD-2s unload on communist troop emplacements along the MLR in 1953. The hilly Korean terrain often had friendly and enemy troops in close proximity, which required an excellent pilot with a stable bombing platform to get the mission done safely. (U.S. Navy)

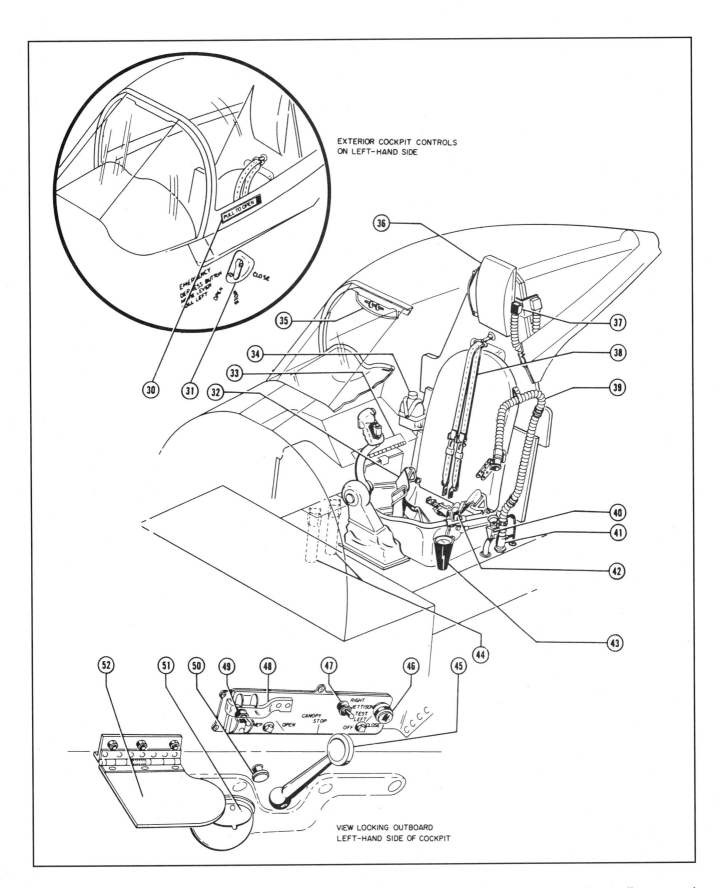

EXTERIOR COCKPIT CONTROLS
ON LEFT-HAND SIDE

PULL TO OPEN

EMERGENCY
DE-PRESS BUTTON
WITH LEVER
PULL LEFT   OPEN   STOP   CLOSE

30 31 32 33 34 35 36 37 38 39 40 41 42 43 44

52 51 50 49 48 47 46 45

RIGHT
JETTISON
TEST
LEFT
OFF   CLOSE

CANOPY
STOP

OPEN

VIEW LOOKING OUTBOARD
LEFT-HAND SIDE OF COCKPIT

The standard Douglas cockpit as delivered had a non-ejectable bucket seat. The canopy was electrically operated by a handle on the left side of the cockpit (#45), and a small switch on the outside of the fuselage (#31). Beginning with the AD-6, the canopy could be ejected. (Larry Davis)

The small radomes on the aft fuselage of this VF-152 Skyraider indicate that it is an AD-2Q (122366), an ECM aircraft with the AN/APA-69 jamming equipment. The AD-2Q held a pair of ECM operators in the rear fuselage as well. (William T. Larkins)

tank on the fuselage centerline and a pair of 300-gallon Mk. 8 external tanks under the wings. Normal range with the three external fuel tanks was in excess of 1,350 miles. With 15 hard points under the wings and fuselage, the XBT2D-1 could carry an awesome total of more than 8,000 pounds of ordnance! This was in addition to the

two M3 20MM cannon mounted in the inboard stub wings. The M3 fired a 5.5-pound projectile at a rate of 400 rounds per minute. The muzzle velocity of the M3 was 2,730 feet per second. The bomb load was equal to that of a Boeing B-17 Flying Fortress, which had four engines.

Several XBT2D-1s were modified for different mission requirements from BuAer. On two aircraft (Bu. No. 09098 and 09099), the interior of the rear fuselage was stripped to make room for two radar operators. This version, XBT2D-1N, was the prototype for a night attack aircraft. The AN/APS-4 radar unit was mounted in a pod under the port

This VA-34 AD-2 was launched from USS Leyte in May 1949 for a firepower demonstration carrying three Mk. 44 torpedoes and twelve 5-inch HVAR rockets— a truly awesome load, uncommon only in that torpedoes were carried. (U.S. Navy)

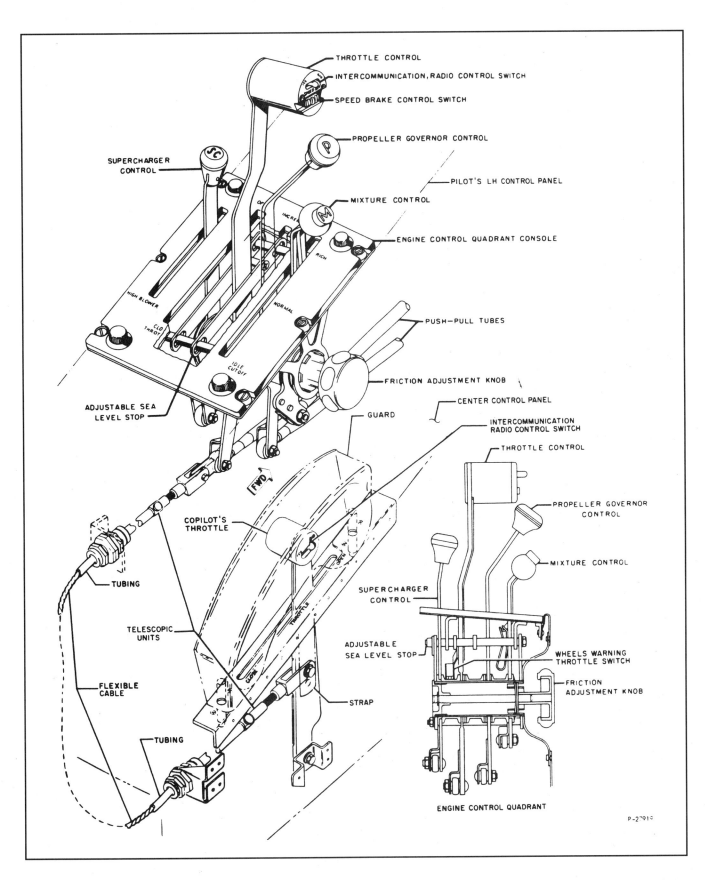

THROTTLE CONTROL

INTERCOMMUNICATION, RADIO CONTROL SWITCH

SPEED BRAKE CONTROL SWITCH

PROPELLER GOVERNOR CONTROL

SUPERCHARGER CONTROL

PILOT'S LH CONTROL PANEL

MIXTURE CONTROL

ENGINE CONTROL QUADRANT CONSOLE

HIGH BLOWER

CLO THROTT

NORMAL

RICH

IDLE CUTOFF

PUSH—PULL TUBES

FRICTION ADJUSTMENT KNOB

ADJUSTABLE SEA LEVEL STOP

CENTER CONTROL PANEL

GUARD

INTERCOMMUNICATION RADIO CONTROL SWITCH

THROTTLE CONTROL

FWD

COPILOT'S THROTTLE

PROPELLER GOVERNOR CONTROL

MIXTURE CONTROL

TUBING

SUPERCHARGER CONTROL

TELESCOPIC UNITS

ADJUSTABLE SEA LEVEL STOP

WHEELS WARNING THROTTLE SWITCH

FLEXIBLE CABLE

STRAP

FRICTION ADJUSTMENT KNOB

TUBING

ENGINE CONTROL QUADRANT

P-27919

The engine controls were on the left console, both for the single-seat and multi-place aircraft. The co-pilot of the two seat AD-5 had a single throttle control on the center console. Radio and dive brake switches were located on the throttle handle. (Larry Davis)

The later variants of the AD-2Q replaced the aft fuselage radomes with multiple blade antennas for the AN/APA-69 ECM jamming equipment. This Marine AD-2Q from VMC-1 is undergoing routine landing gear checks at K-3, Pohang. (U.S. Marine Corps)

An AD-3 from VA-195 aboard USS Princeton *in 1952. The main difference between the AD-2 and the AD-3 was internal wing strengthening. When the wings were folded, it was necessary to install a brace to keep them in place and away from the fuselage.* (Dick Starinchak)

wing, and a large searchlight pod sat under the starboard wing. Squeezing the two radar operators and their equipment into the confines of the rear fuselage necessitated the deletion of the dive brakes on the XBT2D-1N.

The XBT2D-1P (Bu. No. 09096) was a photo reconnaissance version, and the XBT2D-1Q was a prototype electronic countermeasures (ECM) aircraft. The rear fuselage on the -1Q was stripped to make room for two ECM operators and their equipment. An

The pilot of Hefty Betty, *a VA-923 AD-3 (122737), has cranked in full flaps prior to its launch from USS* Bon Homme Richard *in October 1951. Although the ADs could and were often catapulted from the carrier decks, they often launched without using a cat. (John Wood)*

AN/APT-16 ECM radar jamming pod rested under the port wing, and a dispenser pod under the starboard wing showered an enemy radar unit with strips of aluminum foil, a procedure commonly called WINDOW.

Problems with the XBT2D-1 series slowed production greatly. The 13 foot, 6 inch Aeroproducts hollow aluminum propeller generated a serious vibration and the governor was overspeed. Also, the main landing gear and wing support structure began to fail during the Patuxent River service trials. By mid-1946, the landing gear problem had become so acute that Douglas was forced to recall all the in-service XBT2D-1s for wing strengthening. A re-designed landing gear pivot box and heavier wing support area were both incorporated into the AD-1 production run. Testing then continued without further delays.

AD-1 Production

The AD-1 was the first true production variant in the Skyraider series. The first AD-1 (Bu. No. 09110) aircraft made its maiden flight on November 5, 1946. It was identical

Using a hand-powered hoist, Lieutenant Edele, his plane captain and an armament team raise a 1,000-pound M65 bomb into position on the fuselage rack of a VA-923 AD-3 aboard USS Bon Homme Richard *in June 1951. (U.S. Navy)*

An AD-3N (122920) from VC-33 in 1950. The AD-3N was a night attack aircraft equipped with the AN/APS-4 radar pod under its port wing. The radar operator sat in a small compartment behind the pilot, entering the aircraft through the door on the right side. (U.S. Navy)

A VMA-121 AD-3 (122743) sitting ready alert on the ramp at K-3, Pohang, in February 1953. The AD-3 carries twelve 250-pound M57 bombs, and a pair of 110-gallon Mk. 78 Mod 2 fire bombs made from discarded drop tanks. Marine combat squadrons received some of the first AD-3s off the Douglas assembly line. (U.S. Marine Corps)

to the late versions of the XBT2D-1 service test aircraft, with the Wright R-3350-24W engine, the re-designed landing gear and strengthened wing support that had been added to the production requirements after landing gear failures at Patuxent River, and a 365-gallon internal fuel tank. The additional wing strengthening and re-designed landing gear had resulted in an empty weight increase of 415 pounds. But the AD-1 would be the fastest of the production variants with a top speed of 366 MPH. The first Carrier Qualification Trials were flown by VA-4B squadron in April 1947 aboard the *USS Sicily.* Both VA-3B and VA-4B flew their CarQual Tests from the deck of the *Sicily,* although both squadrons were based aboard the *USS Franklin D. Roosevelt,* which was in dry dock at the time.

Douglas built a total of 242 AD-1s before production ceased in August 1949. The remaining 35 aircraft on the original contract of 277, were finished as three-seat ECM models based on the XBT2D-1Q, and were designated AD-1Q. One of the original XBT2D-1s (Bu. No. 09107) was modified for airborne early warning (AEW), with the addition of a large fairing under its fuselage to house an AN/APR-1 radar unit.

This VMA-121 AD-3 (122751) bellied in at K-47, Chunchon, in summer 1952, bending its prop and damaging its lower cowl, oil cooler intake, and landing gear doors. It had been hit over North Korea. The ability of the AD to take a hit and still bring the pilot home made the aircraft legendary in Korea and later in Vietnam. (Ron Picciani)

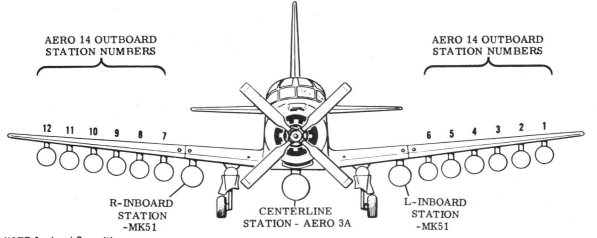

All AD variants had a total of 15 underwing hard points—12 Aero 14 pylons under the outer wing, two Mk. 51 inboard weapons pylons, and an Aero 3A rack on the centerline. Only four of the Aero 14 pylons per wing could hold 500-pound bombs due to space limitations. The Mk. 51 pylon held up to 3,000 pounds of ordnance, while the Aero 3A could handle up to 3,600 pounds of ordnance. (Mac)

Two additional radar operators sat behind and below the pilot in the rear fuselage. The AEW aircraft were strictly defensive in their mission requirements. This prototype aircraft was stripped of all offensive weapons and bombing equipment and designated XAD-1W.

AD-2

The second mass-produced variant of the Skyraider was the AD-2. The AD-2's structure was strengthened even more than the AD-1's had been over the service test aircraft.

Two different prototype aircraft were built: one to test structural improvements and the other as an engine test bed. One of the service test aircraft, XSBT2D-1 Bu. No. 09108, was re-engined with the new Wright R-3350-26W engine, rated at 3,020HP. This engine was slated for use in the AD-2 production aircraft.

The structural strengthening modifications were carried out on one of the middle production AD-1s (Bu. No. 09195). The entire wing was strengthened, with special empha-

sis again on the area of the landing gear bays. Along with the additional strengthening throughout, the AD-2's internal fuel capacity was increased by 15 gallons, for a total of 380 gallons. The cockpit layout changed slightly due to pilot complaints. The main landing gear wells were redesigned from circular with an open wheel, to a square wheel well with gear bay doors. The AD-1 had a small door over the landing gear strut only, leaving the main wheel and tire exposed. All this added weight to the airframe, and its combat weight increased by

In the AD-3W, a pair of radar operators sat below and behind the pilot in a cramped space packed with electronic equipment and radar scopes. The dive brakes were removed to make room for the operators and their equipment. (U.S. Navy)

over 2,700 pounds. Thus the range was reduced in spite of the increase in fuel capacity. Douglas built a total of 156 AD-2s during the 1948 fiscal year.

As with the AD-1, several sub-variants were built using the AD-2 airframe. A few, designated AD-2D., were converted to radio-controlled drone aircraft and used for atom bomb radiation tests. Douglas also built 21 electronic countermeasures aircraft, designated AD-2Q, which held two ECM operators in the rear fuselage. These were built after production of the AD-2 had ceased in the fall of 1948. One aircraft in the middle of the AD-2Q production run (Bu. No. 122373) was modified during production to carry the Mk. 22 tow target system under its fuselage. It was designated AD-2QU.

This VMA-121 AD-3 (BuAer 122800) had recorded over 110 missions against the communists in Korea by the winter of 1952. Three Marine squadrons based in Korea were equipped with various models of AD aircraft. (Ron Picciani)

WARBIRD**TECH**
SERIES

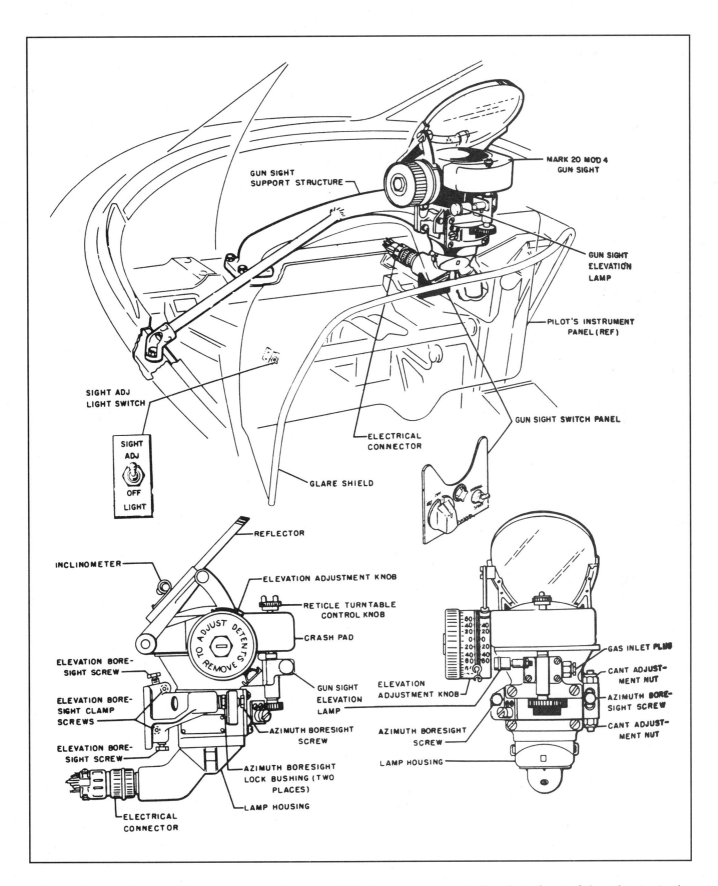

GUN SIGHT SUPPORT STRUCTURE

MARK 20 MOD 4 GUN SIGHT

GUN SIGHT ELEVATION LAMP

PILOT'S INSTRUMENT PANEL (REF)

GUN SIGHT SWITCH PANEL

SIGHT ADJ LIGHT SWITCH

SIGHT ADJ
OFF
LIGHT

ELECTRICAL CONNECTOR

GLARE SHIELD

REFLECTOR

INCLINOMETER

ELEVATION ADJUSTMENT KNOB

RETICLE TURNTABLE CONTROL KNOB

CRASH PAD

TO ADJUST DETENTS TO REMOVE

ELEVATION BORE-SIGHT SCREW

ELEVATION BORE-SIGHT CLAMP SCREWS

ELEVATION BORE-SIGHT SCREW

GUN SIGHT ELEVATION LAMP

AZIMUTH BORESIGHT SCREW

AZIMUTH BORESIGHT LOCK BUSHING (TWO PLACES)

LAMP HOUSING

ELECTRICAL CONNECTOR

GAS INLET PLUG

CANT ADJUSTMENT NUT

AZIMUTH BORESIGHT SCREW

CANT ADJUSTMENT NUT

ELEVATION ADJUSTMENT KNOB

AZIMUTH BORESIGHT SCREW

LAMP HOUSING

The Mark 20 Mod 4 gunsight was mounted on top of the instrument panel, directly in front of the pilot, i.e. in the center of the single-seat variants and over the left instrument panel in the AD-5 two-seat aircraft. The Mark 20 Mod 4 gunsight system was also used in the side-firing AC-47 gunship developed during the Vietnam War. (Mick Roth)

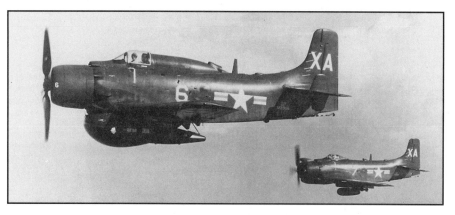

A Navy VX-1 hunter-killer team near Boca Chica, Florida, in January 1950. A team consisted of an AD-3E hunter equipped with the AN/APS-31 air-to-surface radar guppy pod to locate enemy ships, and an AD-3N killer aircraft to attack any that were encountered. The AD-3E was a modified AD-3W with additional vertical tail surfaces on its stabilizers. (U.S. Navy)

AD-3

Following on the heels of the AD-2 series was the even better AD-3. Using the same R-3350-26W engine, the AD-3 had a new propeller and a completely re-designed main landing gear with still greater strength in the gear bay. The main landing gear struts themselves were not only stronger, they also had a 14 inch longer compression stroke on the main landing gear strut, which resulted in less shock to the wing during landings.

Again, the cockpit layout had minor changes as well as a re-designed canopy. As with other improvements, the combat weight increased still more; the AD-3 weighed almost 1,000 pounds more than the AD-2.

The ability of the Douglas engineering team to modify the basic Skyraider design to meet a variety of Navy mission requirements resulted in three major sub-variants in the AD-3 series. Douglas built 15 night attack AD-3Ns based on the

XBT2D-1N, which had the AN/APS-4 radar and searchlight pods under the wings. Following the AD-3Ns off the assembly line were 23 aircraft that were built for the ECM mission and designated AD-3Q. The AD-3Qs were deployed aboard the carriers in detachments of four aircraft each. These aircraft could be quickly modified with the Mk. 22 tow target system that had been developed on the AD-2QU.

The production version of the airborne early-warning Skyraider, which was based on the XAD-1W with an AN/APS-20E search radar housed in a guppy radome under the fuselage, began coming off the assembly line in 1950. The AD-3W housed a pair of additional radar operators in a compartment below and behind the pilot. Externally, the AD-3W had a small pair of vertical fins attached to the stabilizers, a door on the port side for entry into the radar compartment, and a small air scoop atop the fuselage spine to cool the electronic equipment. Douglas built 31 AD-3Ws for the AEW mission.

Finally, the Navy decided that it might be feasible for the Skyraider to perform the anti-submarine mission. Douglas pulled two of the AD-3Ws from the assembly line, removed the AEW guppy radar fairing, and installed the AN/APS-31 Air to Surface Vessel (ASV) search radar in an underwing pod. These aircraft, designated AD-3E, would operate as the search aircraft in a hunter-killer team . Next, a pair of AD-3Ns were modified for the special anti-submarine attack mission and designated AD-3S. Tested in the hunter-killer team mission, the experiment proved highly successful and the requirements were incorporated into the AD-4W series.

The pilot of this VA-35 AD-3 returned to the USS Leyte in November 1950 with a hung 5-inch HVAR rocket, which promptly dropped off as soon as the AD touched the deck. Two Leyte crew members carry the live rocket to the side, where it will be dropped into the ocean. (U.S. Navy)

IMPROVED 2 FIREPOWER

THE AD-4 SERIES

The AD-4 version of the Skyraider was built in greater numbers and more variations than any other variant. The AD-4 used the improved Wright R-3350-26WA engine, which was still rated at 3,020 HP, but it was more economical and dependable than the -26W engine. Other improvements in the AD-4 included a new flat armored windscreen,

a P-1 automatic pilot unit, an improved and strengthened arresting hook assembly, and the ability to use the AN/APS-19A radar, with a Mod 3 or Mod 4 Bombing Director. The prototype aircraft was AD-3, Bu. No. 122853, with a -26WA engine installed. Douglas built 372 AD-4 day attack aircraft before production ceased.

The first of eight sub-variants was the AD-4N, a night attack version with the underwing AN/APS-31 radar pod and Aero 3A searchlight pod. It carried a crew of three—a pilot and two radar operators. The crew entered the radar compartment by either of two small doors on both sides of the fuselage. The AD-4N had a small air scoop on top of the fuselage spine, which provid-

The AD-4 was built in greater numbers than any other variant. The major change from the AD-3 was installation of the R-3350-26WA engine. This AD-4L (BuAer 127352) carries twelve 5-inch HVARs, one 11.75-inch Tiny Tim rocket, and the AN/APS-19 radar pod. The AD-4L was a winterized variant developed for combat in Korea. (Warren Bodie)

Three of the major AD-4 variants fly a demonstration for the Navy brass at NAS LeMoore in 1950. A bombed-up AD-4 leads a night attack AD-4N, trailed by an AD-4W that has an AN/APS-20 guppy pod. (Larry Davis)

An AD-4N (BuAer 126894) assigned to VMC-2 on the flight line at the 1953 Cleveland National Air Race. This AD-4N has the AN/APS-31 radar under its starboard wing, with the Aero 3A searchlight pod under its port wing. Many AD-4s were retrofitted with an additional pair of M3 20MM cannon in the outer wings. (Doug Olsen)

ed cooling air to the electronic equipment in the radar operators position. However, the AD-4N also had pioneered the anti-submarine attack mission along with the AD-3S version. Douglas built a total of 307 AD-4Ns.

The AD-4W was the airborne early warning version, which housed an AN/APS-20 Search Radar in its guppy radome. It also pioneered the anti-submarine search mission with the AD-3E. Douglas built 168 AD-4Ws, 50 of which were transferred to the British Royal Navy and re-designated as the Skyraider AEW-1. Electronic countermeasure duties were handled by the purpose-built AD-4Q, 39 of which were built. The AD-4Q was given the upgraded AN/APT-16 ECM system, based on those units that had been installed on the AD-3Q, and could be quickly identified by the ECM crew entry door on the starboard side of the aircraft.

An AD-4B (BuAer 132362) from VA-75 at NAS North Island in 1953. The AD-4B was the first AD to be able to carry a nuclear weapon. Using a special Mk. 51 weapons' rack on the centerline, the AD-4B could carry, arm, and drop a 1,700-pound Mk. 7 atomic bomb, toss-bombing the device using a Mod 4 Bombing Director. (Jim Sullivan Collection)

The USS Philippine Sea deck crew crowds around VA-115s AD-4s following recovery from the August 1950 morning mission against targets in North Korea. After listening to the pilots talk of results and checking for battle damage, the AD-4s will be re-armed, re-fueled, and re-spotted for the afternoon strike. (U.S. Navy)

An ordnance technician checks the fusing on an M66 2,000-pound bomb aboard USS Princeton *in April 1951. The VA-195 AD-4 also has ten 5-inch RAM rockets, with special warheads to penetrate hard targets, such as railroad tunnels, bridge supports, and bunker complexes. (U.S. Navy)*

Beginning with the AD-4L, several significant changes were brought into the series, most resulting from the on-going combat in Korea. The extreme cold of the Korean winter was causing heavy icing on the combat aircraft operating in the Sea of Japan. Douglas modified 63 standard AD-4s, re-designated AD-4L, with de-icing boots on the leading edges of the wings, stabilizers, and vertical tail, plus anti-icing equipment. At the same time, the offensive firepower of the AD series was doubled with the addition of a second pair of M3 20MM cannons mounted in the outer, folding wing panels. Each gun had 200 rounds in the ammunition bay.

One of the more interesting variations and uses of the AD-4 was that of drone controller, and in a combat environment at that. The Navy had long experimented with remote piloted drone airplanes, both as delivery systems for explosive munitions and as test airplanes used to monitor radiation (AD-2D) during the many surface atomic tests that the United States conducted in the late 1940s. One of the

The USS Princeton *heads back into the Yellow Sea as part of Task Force 77 in 1953. The deck is being re-spotted for recovery operations. A typical Navy air group at this time, would have two squadrons of F9F Panthers, one F4U squadron, and one squadron of ADs. (U.S. Navy)*

One of the most unusual missions of the Korean War was the use of F6F Hellcat drones from GMU-90 loaded with 1,000-pound bombs. The F6Fs had remote controls and television guidance cameras, which were controlled by VC-35 AD-4D drone controllers. One AD-4D controlled the F6F on the deck and during launch. The second waited until the F6F was airborne before taking over control. (Dick Starinchak)

main aircraft types used as a remote drone was the F6F Hellcat.

In the summer of 1952, the Navy put six F6F-5K drones aboard *USS Boxer* for use against communist targets in Korea. The unit responsible for the mission was Guided Missile Unit—90 (GMU-90). Two VC-35 AD-4Ns were modified with drone director equipment giving them the capability to guide the F6F-5Ks to their targets.

The ability of the AD to survive in combat is graphically shown by this AD-4N, which returned to the USS Princeton with 131 holes and missing most of its engine cowling. (U.S. Navy)

One AD-4N would launch from the *Boxer* and move into a position to take over the flight of the F6F-5K. The second AD-4N would stand by on deck as the F6F-5K was moved onto the catapult. The on-deck AD-4N would guide the F6F-5K drone during takeoff and initial climb, where the other AD-4N drone director would take over for the flight to the target. The on-deck AD-4N would then form up with the attack aircraft and proceed to the target as a spare controller.

An AD-4Q prepares to launch from USS Bon Homme Richard in 1950, carrying six 250-pound bombs, two 1,000-pound bombs, and the AN/APT-16 ECM pod. No matter what the designation, the mission of the AD was still that of an attack plane. (John Woods)

WARBIRD**TECH**
S E R I E S

Airplanes BuNo. 134466 through 137632

1. Landing check list
2. Marker beacon light
3. Manifold pressure gage
4. G-2 compass control switch
5. Eight-day clock
6. Airspeed indicator
7. AN/APN-22 radar altimeter
8. Bomb director indicator light
9. G-2 compass caging knob
10. Vertical gyro indicator
11. Gunsight
12. Sight elevation control
13. Search radar scope
14. Standby compass
15. Windshield degrease
16. Fuel quantity test switch
17. Fuel quantity indicator
18. Fuel pressure warning light
19. Take-off check list

20. Carburetor air-free air temperature indicator
21. Outside air temperature switch
21A. Torque pressure gage
22. Deleted
23. Generator warning light
24. Accelerometer
25. Engine gage unit
26. Cylinder head temperature indicator
27. Radio magnetic (course) indicator
28. Rate of climb indicator
28A. Elapsed time clock
29. Rudder pedal adjustment crank
30. Turn and bank (air driven) indicator
30A. Chartboard
31. Altimeter
32. Tachometer
32A. Water injection switch
33. Wheels and flaps position indicator
34. Ignition switch
35. Dive check list

Most Navy and Marine single-seat ADs carried some type of external radar for all-weather bombing. The radar scope was located on the upper right side of the instrument panel. U.S. Air Force and VNAF A-1s did not have a radar bombing system, thus the scope was deleted. (Jim Sullivan)

During an April 1951 strike against a bridge near Wonsan, this VA-195 AD-4 took an accurate anti-aircraft hit, which blew away the tip of its vertical fin and damaged the underside of its wing. But the pilot brought the venerable AD-4 back aboard USS Princeton *for a safe landing. (U.S. Navy)*

The F6F-5K carried a full set of remote-controlled flight systems and a small television camera under its starboard wing and a 2,000-pound bomb on its fuselage bomb rack. As the drone approached the target, the AD-4N controller switched on the television camera, then flew the F6F-5K into the target by looking through the television camera lens. Although not the first robot bombs to be used in combat (both the Army and the Navy had used similar set-ups during World War Two), the GMU-90 Hellcats were the first guided missiles used during the Korean War.

Six GMU-90 missions were flown: the first on August 28, 1952. The target was the Hungnam Bridge. The AD-4N mother ships guided the F6F-5Ks to the target with precision, taking the bridge down with one strike. Other targets included railway bridges and tunnels that had survived many fighter-bomber and B-29 strikes with impunity.

The Navy also called on Douglas to strip 100 of the AD-4N night attack

The AD-4W was an airborne early warning aircraft for fleet defense against enemy air attacks. The AD-4W had the AN/APS-20B search radar in the guppy radome. The AD-4W had a crew of three: a pilot and two radar operators. This AD-4W is assigned to VC-12. (Art Krieger)

This VMC-1 AD-4W, based at Seoul City Airport, K-16, was credited with a PO-2 "Washing Machine Charlie" kill in 1953. The PO-2 biplanes were a very elusive target for the 5th Air Force interceptors, flying so slow and low that the interceptors could not track them. (U.S. Marine Corps)

WARBIRD**TECH**
S E R I E S

The engine cowling of a VA-115 AD-4 opened for full access to the big R-3350 engine. You can see the rear of the special engine mount, designed by Ed Hienemann, and the firewall. The VA-115 AD-4 already had 62 missions recorded on its fuselage side by December 7, 1950. (U.S. Navy)

aircraft of all their night operations equipment, including the additional crew members, so that they could carry an even heavier ordnance load. At the same time, an additional pair of 20MM cannon were installed. These aircraft were designated AD-4NA. Finally, 36 additional AD-4Ns, designated AD-4NL, had de-icing and anti-icing equipment installed, plus the additional 20MM guns.

One final AD-4 variant was produced by Douglas for a special mission— nuclear attack. These aircraft, designated AD-4B, had special stores pylons and strengthened fuselages to carry the Mk. 7 nuclear weapon. A Mk. 51

Landing aboard USS Bon Homme Richard, *the pilot of this VA-65 AD-4 (BuAer 128925) missed the last wire and crashed into an F4U-4 that had been spotted on the front deck. The Corsair was destroyed in the crash, but the AD was reparable. (U.S. Navy)*

This VMC-1 AD-4N has the light gray national insignia and red Modex lettering that was used for night operations during the latter months of the Korean War by Marine Corps squadrons. Named Janet, *the AD-4N was based at K-16, Seoul City Airport. (Charles Trask)*

weapons rack, with an Aero 1A adapter and T-28 weapons saddle, carried the 1,700-pound Mk. 7 atomic bomb on the centerline of the aircraft. With a yield of up to 70 kilotons, it would be necessary for the AD-4B pilot to deliver the bomb using an over-the-shoulder, toss-bombing technique, with an Aero 18C armament control system aided by the Mod 4 Bombing Director. The AD-4B also had the four 20MM cannon armament. The AD-4B was capable of carrying the Mk. 43, Mk. 57, and Mk. 101 Lulu weapons, as well as the Mk. 104 training shapes, commonly called a BLUE BOY.

Douglas modified 28 standard AD-4s to AD-4B specifications, before building 165 production AD-4B aircraft. In May 1953, an AD-4B from VA-301, set a new world record for weight-lifting by a single engine aircraft. Lieutenant Commander J.S. Noonan took off from NAS Dallas with three 1,000-pound bombs, six 750-pound bombs and six 500-pound bombs, plus fuel and 20MM ammunition—a maximum weight of 26,739-pounds, including 14,941 pounds of ordnance. By the end of

The complete air group of USS Boxer *is spotted for launch in the spring of 1951. The ADs will launch first, followed by the faster F4U-4s. The much faster F9F Pantherjets will be launched last, rendezvousing with the other squadrons near the target. (Dick Starinchak)*

Spotted for a launch in the winter of 1951 is the air group aboard USS Bon Homme Richard. *The extreme weather conditions that prevailed in the waters off Korea, resulted in the Navy ordering Douglas to modify over 60 AD-4s with winterizing equipment, including de-icer boots on the wings and tail. The winterized ADs were designated AD-4L.* (Larry Davis)

the production run, Douglas had built a total of 1,051 AD-4s in all its variants.

The first squadron to see combat in the Korean War was VA-55 off the Happy Valley—the *USS Valley Forge.* VA-55's AD-4Qs attacked Pyongyang Airfield on July 3, 1950. It soon became known throughout

Although nose art was not generally found on Navy/Marine aircraft, many did carry personal names and sayings. Betty Lou, an AD-4Q, flew with VF-54 aboard USS Essex *in the fall of 1951. The performance of the AD was so superb, that the Navy had two AD squadrons originally tasked with a fighter mission.* (V.A. Fleming)

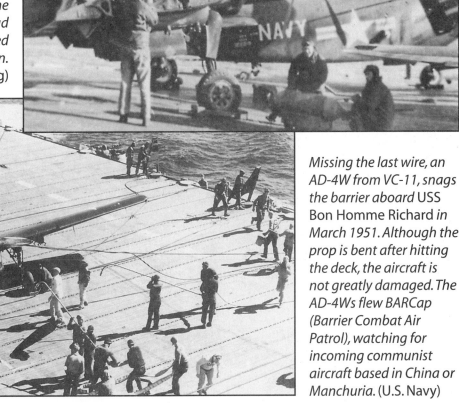

Missing the last wire, an AD-4W from VC-11, snags the barrier aboard USS Bon Homme Richard *in March 1951. Although the prop is bent after hitting the deck, the aircraft is not greatly damaged. The AD-4Ws flew BARCap (Barrier Combat Air Patrol), watching for incoming communist aircraft based in China or Manchuria.* (U.S. Navy)

As the AD was replaced by Grumman A-6 Intruder jet attack aircraft, they were transferred to Naval Air Reserve squadrons. This NAR Atlanta AD-4 undergoes major maintenance at Peachtree Airport, Atlanta, Georgia, in August 1967. It has the International Orange fuselage band, indicating an aircraft with a reserve squadron. (Douglas)

the Korean Theater that the ADs were probably carrying everything but the kitchen sink. In fact, one AD pilot off the *USS Boxer* strapped a sink to a 500-pound bomb, which was dropped on a target in North Korea. The normal load for an AD operating over Korea was over 3,000 pounds.

In late 1950, the ADs were armed with aerial torpedoes for a special mission. They were going to hit the gates of the Hwachon Dam, which had withstood repeated attacks by bombing. Three torpedoes from the ADs brought the dam down.

During the Korean War, the Navy and Marine ADs' performance was flawless, quite often bordering on amazing. The Navy ordnance crews were heard to complain that "the AD just carries too damn much!" One of the often told stories about the ability of the AD occurred when an Army Forward Air Controller (FAC) contacted a flight of ADs.

The pilot of this VA-42 AD-6 performs a classic bolter after missing the last wire aboard USS Forrestal *during March 1956 maneuvers near Cuba. The 3,000 HP R-3350 engine made such maneuvers seem routine. One of the AD-6 improvements was a hydraulically operated tail hook, and all AD-6s had four M3 20MM cannons. (U.S. Navy)*

A VA-25 AD-6 (134488) takes off from USS Independence *in July 1959 carrying a pair of 250-pound practice bombs and two 150-gallon drop tanks. Although the Navy changed to the gray and white tactical paint scheme in 1957, this 1959 photo proves that it takes time to repaint all those aircraft. (Jim Sullivan Collection)*

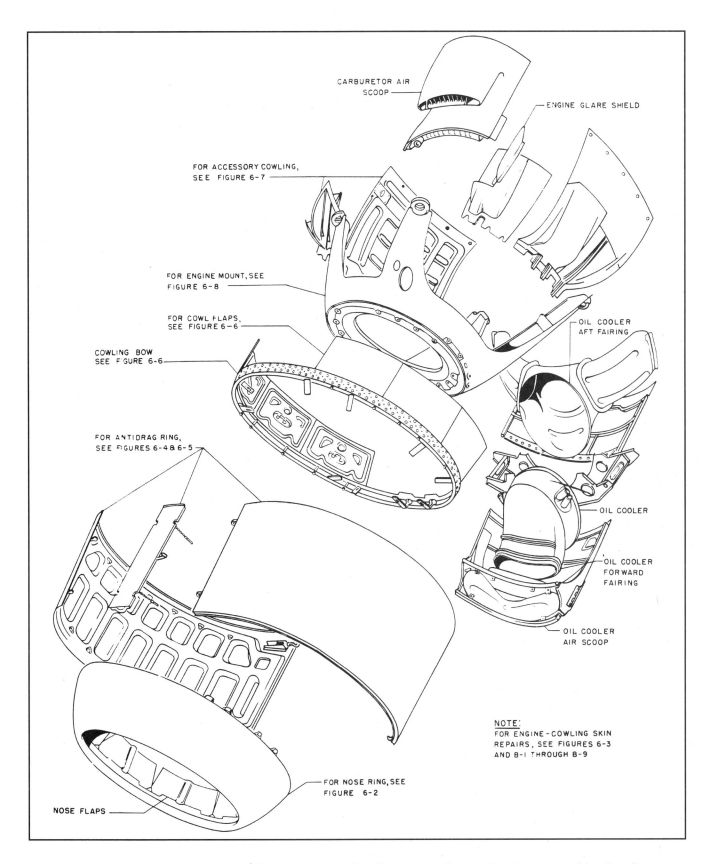

CARBURETOR AIR SCOOP

ENGINE GLARE SHIELD

FOR ACCESSORY COWLING, SEE FIGURE 6-7

FOR ENGINE MOUNT, SEE FIGURE 6-8

FOR COWL FLAPS, SEE FIGURE 6-6

COWLING BOW SEE FIGURE 6-6

FOR ANTIDRAG RING, SEE FIGURES 6-4 & 6-5

OIL COOLER AFT FAIRING

OIL COOLER

OIL COOLER FORWARD FAIRING

OIL COOLER AIR SCOOP

NOTE:
FOR ENGINE-COWLING SKIN REPAIRS, SEE FIGURES 6-3 AND B-1 THROUGH B-9

FOR NOSE RING, SEE FIGURE 6-2

NOSE FLAPS

The engine cowling and mount assembly was the same for all variants. The cowl had two sets of cooling flaps: one set at the rear of the cowl or anti-drag ring, and another set of flaps inside the nose ring. Both sets of flaps could be manually operated by the pilot or automatically controlled with actuation of the landing gear. Air Force A-1s had the nose ring flaps fixed in the open position for greater cooling in the heat of Southeast Asia. (Mick Roth)

The Marine Corps began receiving AD-6s in 1954. This AD-6 is assigned to VMA-332 at MCAS Miami, Florida, and clearly shows the typical exhaust pattern of the R-3350. The light-colored area in front of the windscreen is actually the faded, flat-black anti-glare panel. (USMC)

FAC Pilot: "I have a possible target for you. Troops and tanks. What kind of ordnance do you guys have?" The AD Leader answered rather matter-of-factly: "Each aircraft has three 1000-pound bombs and twelve 5-inch HVAR rockets." FAC Pilot: "Yah, right. You guys are full of bull. No single engine airplane can carry that kind of load!" Well, maybe not an Army plane.

In Korea, the ADs proved that they could take it, as well as dish it out. One AD took a 40MM anti-aircraft shell through the bottom of its fuselage, exploding eight feet behind the pilot. Another took a hit in the starboard stub wing, exploding its 20MM cannon and all of the ammunition, leaving a huge hole in the wing just inboard of the fold.

A VA-196 AD-6 (134564) taxis to a parking spot on the foredeck of USS Lexington in July 1957 after recovery from a practice mission in the Gulf of Mexico. Its Navy tail code letters indicate the carrier air group, but not necessarily the aircraft carrier assignment. VA-196 painted the entire wing leading edges in its squadron color—red. (U.S. Navy)

Lieutenant (Junior Grade) William Barron, a VA-95 AD pilot aboard USS Princeton, took a 37MM hit in the tail area over Ambyon, blowing an 18-inch hole in the tail and more than 200 shrapnel holes in the aircraft's rear fuselage. All three of these aircraft returned safely to their carriers and flew again.

An AD-6 (137612) from VA-125 with CVG-12 in 1957, wears the new Light Grey (F.S. 36440) and white tactical paint. The very small tail codes and oversize national insignia are part of the evolution of Navy and Marine aircraft markings during the paint changeover. (Paul Vercammen)

A VA-75 AD-6 aerial tanker is chained down to the deck of USS Independence *in July 1961. The 300-gallon centerline fuel tank of a tanker aircraft came with a drogue hose and winch assembly, which the pilot deployed to refuel other aircraft. The nose flaps inside the engine cowling are in the fully closed position.* (U.S. Navy)

AD-6

The AD-6 was a combination of the AD-4B's traits and the improvements called for in the AD-5 series. The AD-6 had all the additional strengthening found on previous variants. This included skin doublers in the wheel wells, strengthening of the entire wing structure in the area of the landing gear, and re-enforced skin over the wing above the landing gear. This allowed the AD-6 pilot to have a sink rate of up to 23 feet per second, almost twice that designed into the original AD-1 requirements. The AD-6 also had the revised bomb racks that had been developed for the AD-5 series, including the forward swept underwing tank pylons, a jettisonable canopy, hydraulically raised tail hook assembly, improved cockpit layout and a revised lighting system. The AD-6 also had a nuclear attack capability, and it incorporated the Mod 4 Bombing Director that had been necessary on the AD-4B nuclear attack mission. The AD-6 was capable of firing the AGM-12A or -12B Bullpup missile.

A VA-75 AD-6 (139804) just prior to touch down aboard USS Independence *in October 1962. The AD-6 had a sink rate of 23 feet per second during a carrier landing— best described as a controlled crash!* (U.S. Navy)

An AD-6 (139632) from VMA-225 on the ramp at MCAS Cherry Point carries a Mk. 7 nuclear bomb shape, called a Blue Boy due to its color. The Mk. 7 weapon had a folding ventral fin for ground clearance. It is not generally known that the Marine Corps had a nuclear mission. (Jim Sullivan Collection)

During the Vietnam War, with the SAM threat growing all the time, The Navy developed an ALQ-81 ECM pod, which could be carried on the centerline of the A-1H or J. One of the most important additions to the AD-6 series, especially to the pilots who would fly over Vietnam, was the addition of armor plate to the fuselage sides and the bottom around the cockpit. Douglas built 713 AD-6 aircraft. There were no sub-variant types like those found in the AD-4 series.

AD-7

The final production version of the single-seat Skyraider was the AD-7. The AD-7 had the improved R-3350-26WB engine and strengthened landing gear. The installation of the additional pair of 20MM cannons had caused a fatigue problem in the outer wing panels of the AD-4/AD-6 series, so they were also strengthened. Along with the new engine, the engine mounts were strengthened and re-designed. The AD-7 also had a nuclear capability. Both the AD-6 and AD-7 could carry the new multiple ejector

A VA-196 A-1H (139735) from USS Bon Homme Richard is about to land at NAS Atsugi, Japan, in the summer of 1964. The Department of Defense changed the designation of the AD-6 to A-1H in September 1962. The inside of the drop tanks have been painted flat black as an anti-glare measure. (Niromichi Gabari)

An AD-6 wearing the colorful markings of VA-145 Swordsmen near Hawaii when they were assigned to USS Hornet. The Swordsmen converted to AD-6s in February 1956. The nose scallops, lightning bolt, tail, and wing leading edges were painted bright green. (U.S. Navy)

An A-1H from VA-145 exhibits the classic lines of the Skyraider at rest. In the late 1950s, an anti-collision beacon was added to the tip of the tail and under the fuselage on all AD aircraft. The A-1H had the new Mk. 51 wing pylons and Aero 14 bomb racks. (Jim Sullivan Collection)

racks (MERs), each of which would hold six bombs, on the Mk. 51 bomb pylons. Douglas only built 72 AD-7s, with the 3,180th and final Skyraider, Bu. No. 142081, coming off the El Segundo, California, assembly line on February 18, 1957. to be delivered to VA-215.

A major change in the appearance of all Skyraiders took effect in August 1957, when BuAer changed the basic color scheme of all Navy aircraft from Glossy Sea Blue (F.S. 15042) to Gull Grey (F.S. 36440) upper surfaces, with a gloss white underside. Then in September 1962, the Department of Defense called for a re-designation of major weapons systems within the armed services. All the Skyraiders became A-1s, with the AD-4 becoming the A-1D, the AD-6 becoming the A-1H, and the AD-7 becoming the A-1J.

Skyraider flight training was conducted at the VA-122 Spad School, which was initially based at North Island NAS, then at Moffett Field, before finally being transferred to NAS LeMoore. Strangely, the main overhaul depot for the AD was at NAS Quonset Point, Rhode Island. The AD Skyraider was the main

An AD-6 from VA-65 aboard USS Intrepid *taxis to the forward deck after recovering in 1960. Atlantic carrier air groups had tail codes beginning with the letter "A." The dark stripe on its wing is a black anti-skid walkway. (Dick Starinchak)*

A pair of AD-6s assigned to the Marine Corps Reserve Squadron, AES-12, at MCAS Quantico, Virginia, in November 1959. Navy and Marine reserve squadron aircraft carried colorful paint jobs, with International Orange trailing edges on all flying surfaces and the bottom of the fuselage. (USMC)

Shush Boomer, *an A-1H (BuAer 135272) assigned to VA-165 aboard* USS Intrepid *on Yankee Station in September 1966, taxis onto the port catapult with a load of Mk. 82 500-pound Low Drag General Purpose (LDGP) bombs, fitted with Snake-eye fins to retard the bomb drop speed. Ensign James Star has 23 missions recorded on the side of* Shush Boomer. *(Dick Starinchak)*

attack aircraft used by the U.S. Navy and Marine Corps. During 1955 to '57, no less than 42 squadrons were in active service—29 with the Navy and another 13 with the Marines. By the early 1960s, though, the time of the propeller-driven attack plane was drawing to a close; the Navy also wanted an all-jet air fleet. In 1963, VA-75 became the first AD squadron to transition into the new Grumman A-6A Intruder jet attack aircraft.

VIETNAM

The old Spad still had plenty of time to see another round of action. This time in some country named Vietnam. When President Johnson ordered the first strikes

On June 20, 1965, Lieutenant Clint Johnson, a VA-25 pilot flying A-1H BuAer 139768 from USS Midway, *was credited with 1/2 a victory when he and Lieutenant Charles Harman shot down a North Vietnamese MiG-17 attempting to break up a search and rescue effort 50 miles northwest of Than Hoa, North Vietnam. (Jim Sullivan Collection)*

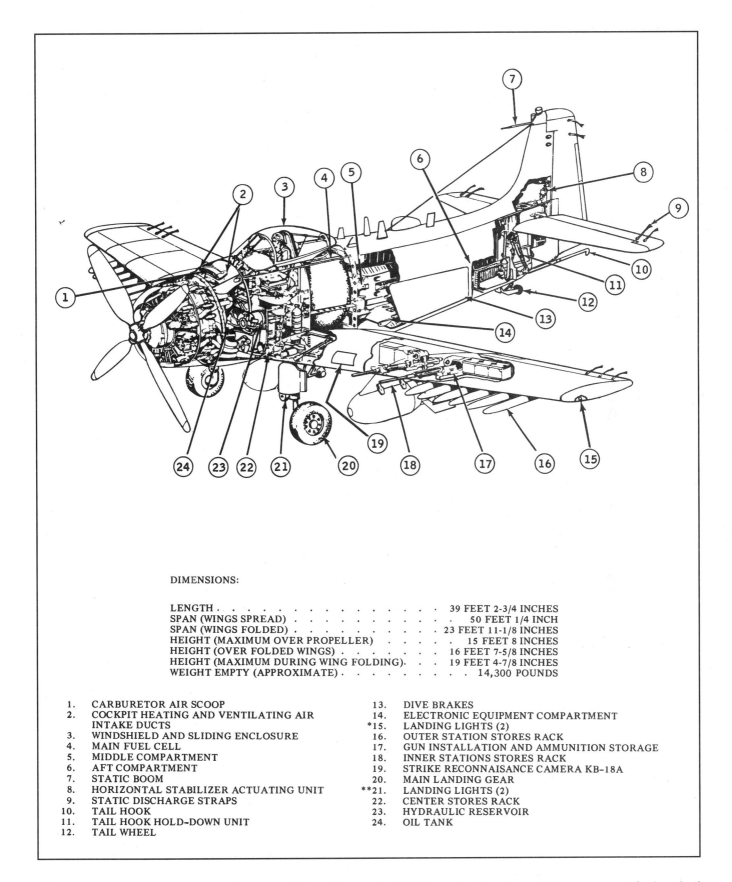

DIMENSIONS:

LENGTH . . . . 39 FEET 2-3/4 INCHES
SPAN (WINGS SPREAD) . . . . 50 FEET 1/4 INCH
SPAN (WINGS FOLDED) . . . . 23 FEET 11-1/8 INCHES
HEIGHT (MAXIMUM OVER PROPELLER) . . . . . 15 FEET 8 INCHES
HEIGHT (OVER FOLDED WINGS) . . . . 16 FEET 7-5/8 INCHES
HEIGHT (MAXIMUM DURING WING FOLDING). . . 19 FEET 4-7/8 INCHES
WEIGHT EMPTY (APPROXIMATE) . . . . 14,300 POUNDS

1.	CARBURETOR AIR SCOOP	13.	DIVE BRAKES
2.	COCKPIT HEATING AND VENTILATING AIR	14.	ELECTRONIC EQUIPMENT COMPARTMENT
	INTAKE DUCTS	*15.	LANDING LIGHTS (2)
3.	WINDSHIELD AND SLIDING ENCLOSURE	16.	OUTER STATION STORES RACK
4.	MAIN FUEL CELL	17.	GUN INSTALLATION AND AMMUNITION STORAGE
5.	MIDDLE COMPARTMENT	18.	INNER STATIONS STORES RACK
6.	AFT COMPARTMENT	19.	STRIKE RECONNAISANCE CAMERA KB–18A
7.	STATIC BOOM	20.	MAIN LANDING GEAR
8.	HORIZONTAL STABILIZER ACTUATING UNIT	**21.	LANDING LIGHTS (2)
9.	STATIC DISCHARGE STRAPS	22.	CENTER STORES RACK
10.	TAIL HOOK	23.	HYDRAULIC RESERVOIR
11.	TAIL HOOK HOLD-DOWN UNIT	24.	OIL TANK
12.	TAIL WHEEL		

General arrangement cut-away drawing of the Air Force A-1H/J shows the location of the armament, fuel and oil tanks. With the exception of the antenna array, the Air Force and Navy / Marine A-1s were identical. The dimensions are the same for all single-seat variants from AD-1 through AD-7 (A-1J). (Mac)

The deck of USS Intrepid is a very busy place prior to another strike against targets in North Vietnam during February 1966. The Intrepid was an anti-submarine warfare support carrier, that flew search and rescue missions while on Yankee Station. The A-1Hs are assigned to VA-176. The first aircraft has open nose flaps, while the second aircraft's are closed. (U.S. Navy)

A Pair of VA-215 A-1Hs form up off the wingtip of an Air Force HU-16 Albatross flying boat during a Combat Search and Rescue (CSAR) mission into the Gulf of Tonkin in 1966. Navy A-1s were the primary CSAR support aircraft for water rescues and rescue missions in eastern and southern North Vietnam. (Tom Hansen)

against the North Vietnamese torpedo boat bases in retaliation for the Tonkin Gulf Incident, it would be Navy A-1s that performed the task. The Navy put two carrier task groups on-station for operations over Vietnam. One carrier off the coast of South Vietnam, known as Dixie Station. In the Gulf of Tonkin, as many as three attack carriers were on Yankee Station. The flight crews on Yankee Station flew missions into North Vietnam and Laos.

On August 5, 1964, A-1Hs from VA-52 aboard *USS Ticonderoga*, supported by A-1s from VA-145 aboard *USS Constellation*, attacked the North Vietnamese torpedo boat bases as part of Operation Rolling Thunder. It was, however, not without cost, as the NVA gunners shot down one VA-145 A-1H (Bu. No. 139760) during that very first raid. Lieutenant (Junior Grade) R.C. Sather was the first Navy pilot killed in action during the Vietnam War.

In 1966, the Navy began to experiment with camouflage colors for tactical aircraft involved in the Vietnam War. A-1 aircraft were painted two greens over their upper surfaces. The experiment was not a success, and one of VA-115s A-1Hs, shown, still had a badly worn camouflage at NAS Quonset Point in August 1968. (Jim Sullivan Collection)

(Above) Lieutenant Commander Ed Greathouse flew Paper Tiger II, *a VA-25 A-1H aboard* USS Midway *in late 1965. Greathouse prepares to takeoff with an unusual ordnance load. I wonder what the ballistics are for a toilet? Greathouse was Canasta Lead on the MiG-killer flight of June 20, and has over 120 missions recorded on the fuselage. (JEM Aviation Slide)*

The very, very weathered paint evident on the upper wing of this VA-152 "Aces" A-1H is a clear indication of the rough conditions aboard a carrier on Yankee Station during the war. The deck officer aboard USS Oriskany is about ready to signal the pilot to stop engine after he has him spotted for parking. The black spots on the leading edge of the wing are antennae. (U.S. Navy)

This VA-25 A-1H aboard USS Coral Sea *in August 1967 has obviously just returned from North Vietnam as indicated by the very heavy gun smudging around all four 20*MM *cannons. Each M3 20*MM *cannon had a magazine holding 200 rounds. (Don Jay)*

Commander Jim Ehret's VA-25 A-1H (139779) flies with flaps and gear down so the A-1 can keep formation with an Air Force HU-16B Albatross flying boat during a Combat Search and Rescue (CSAR) mission. Air Force Hu-16s based at DaNang were often supported by Navy A-1 CSAR flights. The extremely worn paint on the upper surfaces is typical of aircraft on Yankee Station. (Tom Hansen)

WARBIRD**TECH**
S E R I E S

A pair of VA-145 A-1Hs off the USS Constellation on Dixie Station in 1965. The NK-506 is armed with a pair of M65 1,000-pound bombs and two M57 500-pound bombs, while NK-511 has LAU-6 rocket pods in addition to bombs for an armed reconnaissance strike in South Vietnam. (U.S. Navy)

However, the old A-1 exacted a toll on all kinds of North Vietnamese weaponry, including their air force. On June 20, 1965, Canasta Flight from VA-25 aboard the *USS Midway*, was "feet dry" as part of a CSAR (Combat Search & Rescue) mission into North Vietnam, when it was jumped by two North Vietnamese MiG-17 jets. The MiGs succeeded in forcing the A-1s to jettison their ordnance and go defensive with what is commonly called a Lufberry circle. In a Lufberry, the flight of A-1s just flew in a continuous circle, with each pilot covering the other's tail.

The MiGs also flew in tight circles, trying to get a clear shot at one of the A-1s. One of the MiGs made a fatal mistake and attempted to break through the Lufberry to hit the A-1 on the other side. As the MiG lost energy and speed, it flew directly in front of Lieutenant Clint Johnson's A-1H—and his four 20mm cannons! Johnson and Lieutenant Charles Hartman used a classic scissors maneuver, putting the MiG-17 between both aircraft. Whichever way the MiG broke, one of the two

Canasta Flight from VA-25 aboard USS Midway in 1965. Lieutenant Commander Greathouse (NE-570) leads, followed by Lieutenant (junior grade) J.S. Lynn (NE 571), Lieutenant Clint Johnson (NE 577), and Lieutenant Charles Hartman (NE-575). Lieutenants Johnson and Hartman shared a MiG-17 victory on June 20, 1965. (U.S. Navy)

A veteran VA-145 A-1H (135338) from the USS Constellation in 1966. The badge on the rear fuselage, above the word "NAVY," is the "Tonkin Gulf Yacht Club" insignia worn by Navy crews that operated on Yankee Station during the Vietnam War. (Mike Grove)

A-1Hs had a good shot at him. First Johnson, then Hartman's 20MM cannons ripped into the MiG-17, which fell off to the right and into the jungle. Lieutenants Johnson and Hartman were each given credit for 1/2 of the MiG-17 kill.

And to prove that it was no fluke, Lieutenant (Junior Grade) W.T. Patton, an A-1H driver assigned to VA-176, shot down another North Vietnamese MiG on November 11, 1966. Patton was Papoose 409 and was inbound toward a target in Route Pak 5, when he suddenly saw a North Vietnamese MiG-17 jump on another A-1 flying about 3,000 feet below him. Patton jettisoned his ordnance and tanks and rolled over, diving down on the MiG. The MiG broke off its attack on the other A-1, pulled up and started a hard climbing left turn, trying to get away from the rapidly closing American above him. Patton closed to within 200 feet before the MiG could accelerate away. Patton opened fire

An interesting before and after series of photos shows Commander Cliff Church checking the arming wires of the Mk. 82 500-pound Low Drag General Purpose bombs (LDGP) and Zuni rocket pods under the right wing of his aircraft Jefferson Airplane. *Under the left wing is an Mk. 82, bearing graffiti, with an 18-inch fuse extender. Finally, Church returns to the* USS Midway *with empty bomb racks and Zuni pods. The* Airplane *was assigned to Church when he commanded VA-25 in 1968. The metal tabs above the exhausts shielded the pilot's eyes during night flights. (Dick Starinchak)*

WARBIRDTECH
SERIES

This VA-176 A-1H (137543) was flown by Lieutenant (Junior Grade) W. Thomas Patton when he shot down a North Vietnamese MiG-17 on November 1, 1966. The aircraft is shown at NAS Quonset Point in August 1968 as VA-176 was beginning the transition into the A-7 Corsair II. (Jim Sullivan Collection)

The last combat launch by a VA-115 Arabs A-1H from the deck of USS Kitty Hawk was commemorated by the crews, who added graffiti markings to the aircraft fuselage. On Yankee Station at the time, the Arab deck crews used only the proper color for the markings—bright green, which was the same as the squadron color. (via Jeff Ethell)

Typical of Navy personal markings in the combat zone is an appropriately named King of the Load, a VA-165 A-1H aboard USS Intrepid in October 1966. Commander Harry Parode has at least 66 mission credits on the fuselage of the King (note the single bomb with "50"). Nose art was virtually non-existent with Navy squadrons. (Walt Ohrlich)

The AD-7 was the final Skyraider variant mass-produced by Douglas. Production of the A-1 series was halted after 72 AD-7s had been built, on February 18, 1957. This AD-7 (142056) was assigned to VA-122, the A-1 replacement training unit; its Day-Glo Orange wing and tail bands indicate a training aircraft. (Jim Sullivan Collection)

A VA-52 A-1J from the USS Ticonderoga *recovers at DaNang, South Vietnam, following a CSAR mission into southern North Vietnam in 1966. The AD-7 designation was changed to A-1J in September 1962. (Tom Hansen)*

with the four 20MM cannons, getting many solid hits on the MiG-17 fuselage. The MiG immediately went out of control in an inverted position, and the MiG driver punched out of his crippled jet.

So much for the theory that the old Skyraider couldn't hold her own in a jet war. But the handwriting was on the wall, especially when the North Vietnamese began locating surface-to-air missile launchers around all the major targets in North Vietnam. On April 13, 1966, a SAM destroyed a VA-52 A-1H, and another A-1H from VA-25 was downed by one of the Soviet-built missiles on September 14, 1966. The old Spad was a sitting duck in the missile war. On February 20, 1968, Lieutenant (Junior Grade) Ted Hill made the last combat landing by a Navy A-1 Skyraider, when his VA-25 A-1H (Bu. No. 135300) touched down on the deck of *USS Coral Sea.* On April 10, 1968, the Navy officially retired the A-1 in a ceremony at NAS LeMoore, home of the Spad School. With a final "Farewell and well done," Lieutenant (Junior

A VA-196 A-1J is ready for launch using the starboard catapult on USS Bon Homme Richard *on Dixie Station in 1965. The Flying Devils A-1J carries four M117 750-pound bombs and a pair of the 300-gallon Mk. 8 drop tanks. (Jim Sullivan Collection)*

An A-1J from VA-25 drops 500-pound bombs on a target in South Vietnam in 1965. From Dixie Station off the coast of South Vietnam, Navy A-1s, such as this aircraft from USS Midway, *could hit targets almost anywhere in South Vietnam and Laos. (U.S. Navy)*

A VA-165 A-1J (142059) from USS Intrepid, on the ramp at DaNang in September 1966, shows 55 missions on its fuselage side. The A-1J could be fitted with the aerial tanker kit, just like all the A-1 variants. This A-1J had an in-flight problem, which caused it to recover in-country at DaNang. (Mike Jennings)

The last A-1J built by Douglas was No. 142081. It is seen here at Quonset Point in 1965 when it was assigned to VA-122, the Spad School. This aircraft was the last of 3,180 A-1s that had been built by Douglas. (Jim Sullivan Collection)

Grade) Hill made a last flyby, followed by a flight of A-4 Skyhawks. An era of Navy history was over.

With the end of the Skyraider war in Vietnam, it was time to tally up the score. U.S. Navy A-1 operations had begun in August 1964, continuing through Lieutenant (Junior Grade) Hill's final launch from the USS Coral Sea on February 20, 1968. The A-1s on Yankee and Dixie Stations flew a grand total of 31,105 combat sorties, 19,809 of them going into North Vietnam, home of the fiercest air defense system in history. Between the radar-directed anti-aircraft fire and the SAMs, 303 A-1s were hit, 42 of those aircraft subsequently were shot down over North and South Vietnam. EA-1 operations added another 6,842 combat sorties to the total. Enemy gunners hit four of the EA-1s, and one of those was shot down.

VA-25 A-1Js prepare to unfold their wings prior to launch from the USS Coral Sea in 1968 on a ResCAP mission into North Vietnam. NL-414 carries LAU-10A Zuni rocket pods. Navy SAR aircraft flying from Yankee Station, could not carry the ordnance loads of the Air Force A-1s, which were based much closer to the combat arena. (U.S. Navy)

WARBIRDTECH
SERIES

SIDE BY SIDE

The AD-5 was Douglas' answer to the Navy requirement for an advanced anti-submarine aircraft. Recall that the anti-submarine versions of ADs were all projected as hunter-killer teams with AD-3E hunters and AD-3S killers, which were later combined with the AD-4W and AD-4N missions. Douglas proposed to build an advanced AD with side-by-side seating, which would combine the hunter-killer team mission into a single aircraft. The new design would be the AD-5.

Using an AD-4, Bu. No. 124006, as its prototype, Douglas widened the fuselage out to the edge of the wingroot, then added 9 inches to the width for good measure. The widening took place between the wing leading edge and trailing edge, before tapering back to the tail area. The widened cockpit housed two pilots in the front, with full flight instruments; leaving room for a pair of radar operators or other personnel in the rear. As with

(Above) This AD-4 124006 was modified with a wide-body fuselage, creating the prototype for the AD-5. The AD-5 had the early-style wing with open landing gear bays. It also had an 11-inch increase in fuselage length and a much larger vertical fin area. (Douglas Aircraft Co.)

Two variations of the AD-5 in formation with an AD-4W from VMC-2: CM-21 is an AD-5Q with the AN/APS-16 ECM pod under its right wing; while CM-10 is an AD-5W with the AN/APS-20B search radar in a guppy radome. The AD-5Q retained an offensive bombing capability, while the AD-5W did not. (U.S. Marine Corps)

The AD-5N was a night attack version using the AN/APS-31 radar in a pod under the starboard wing. Under the port wing is the Aero 3B searchlight / sonobuoy / flare dispenser pod. This AD-5N was assigned to VC-33 Night Hawks in 1952. (Jim Sullivan Collection)

other AD types that carried additional personnel in the rear, the fuselage side dive brakes were eliminated to make room for the additional crew and their equipment. The underside or ventral dive brake was retained.

In addition to the widening of the fuselage, it was also lengthened 1 foot, 11 inches in the area of the new rear cockpit, moving the engine forward 8 inches. The vertical tail surfaces were increased over 50 percent in area, although it was only 2 actual inches taller in height than the single-seat variants. The wingspan was the same as previous variants, even with the widened fuselage. All other improvements that had been incorporated into the single-seat versions, i.e. re-designed and strengthened landing gear and air frame, an additional pair of 20MM cannon, and the improved bomb racks, all went into the production versions of the AD-5.

The AD-5 mockup was inspected and approved in October 1950, and the prototype made a first flight on August 17, 1951. The Navy was so excited about the AD-5 and all its

The AD-5 had complete offensive combat capabilities, the same as all single-seat AD variants, including 12 Aero 14 underwing hard points for bomb carriage or rocket launchers, a centerline station, and the new Mk. 51 pylons, which could carry the 11.75-inch Tiny Tim rockets. This AD-5 (133926) is from VMA-332. (Jim Sullivan Collection)

This UA-1E (133907) was assigned to VAW-33 Night Hawks aboard USS Essex in 1964. The AD-5 was re-designated A-1E in September 1962. A UA-1E is a utility aircraft and target tug, painted dark gray with yellow wings and an orange tail. (Roger Besecker)

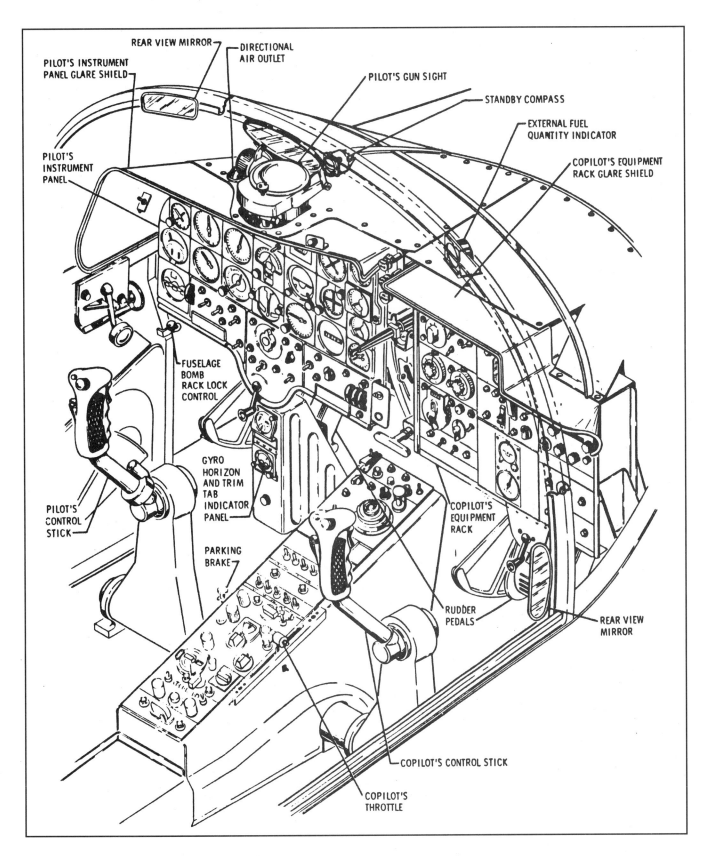

REAR VIEW MIRROR

DIRECTIONAL AIR OUTLET

PILOT'S INSTRUMENT PANEL GLARE SHIELD

PILOT'S GUN SIGHT

STANDBY COMPASS

EXTERNAL FUEL QUANTITY INDICATOR

PILOT'S INSTRUMENT PANEL

COPILOT'S EQUIPMENT RACK GLARE SHIELD

FUSELAGE BOMB RACK LOCK CONTROL

GYRO HORIZON AND TRIM TAB INDICATOR PANEL

PILOT'S CONTROL STICK

COPILOT'S EQUIPMENT RACK

PARKING BRAKE

RUDDER PEDALS

REAR VIEW MIRROR

COPILOT'S CONTROL STICK

COPILOT'S THROTTLE

The cockpit arrangement for the multi-place AD-5 series had flight instruments on the left side for the pilot only. The co-pilot panel had the navigational and radar bombing equipment. The co-pilot's control stick could be completely removed and stored behind the seat on Air Force A-1Es and Gs. The center console had radio controls, starter and primer switches for the pilot, and the co-pilot's throttle. (Mick Roth)

An EA-1E/A-1H hunter-killer team shows the vast differences between the fuselage contours of the two variants. The clear cockpit canopy over the rear cockpit of the EA-1E has been replaced with a metal door with small windows for instrument clarity. (U.S. Navy)

possible uses, that it quickly ordered 212 standard day attack aircraft. One of the things that excited the Navy brass was the ability to change the mission of the AD-5 through installation of various kits to meet the requirements of a variety of secondary missions. Removal of the radar and ECM equipment left a very large space in which to carry troops, VIPs, or equipment. The AD-5 could also serve as a flying ambulance, holding up to four litters. As a transport aircraft, the AD-5 could be fitted with four rearward facing seats. The AD-5 could also be outfitted with a five-camera reconnaissance package or be used as a transport, hauling up to 2,000 pounds of cargo. One of the kits even included a built-in hoist for lifting the cargo into the aircraft. Douglas built 212 AD-5 day attack aircraft.

The large rear cockpit area lent itself easily to many sub-variants, such as the night attack AD-5N, with Aero 3B searchlight / Sonobuoy / flare dispenser and AN/APS-31 radar pods under the wings. Douglas built 239 AD-5Ns for the Navy and Marines.

The AD-5W was the anti-submarine version. An AN/APS-20B anti-submarine radar was housed in a large, bulbous radome under the forward fuselage; it looked like a pregnant guppy in flight. The glass rear canopy was replaced by a metal unit with two small windows. The AD-5W usually had no underwing pylons for ordnance, except for the pair used to carry underwing drop tanks. Douglas built a total of 218 AD-5Ws, which were deployed aboard the carriers in detachments of four aircraft.

The AD-5Q was an electronic countermeasures aircraft that had the AN/APS-16 ECM transmitter pod, with two ECM operators in the rear cockpit. Douglas built 53 AD-5Q conversion kits, which could be installed in AD-5N air frames. All ECM missions were handled by one squadron for the Atlantic Fleet and one squadron in the Pacific, again with four-aircraft detachments aboard the carriers. The Department of Defense re-designation program in September 1962 saw the AD-5 daylight attack aircraft re-designated as the A-1E, the AD-5N became the A-1G, the AD-5W became the EA-1E, and the AD-5Q became the EA-1F.

An EA-1E (135018) from VAW-33 rests on the transient aircraft ramp at RAF Luga on the island of Malta in March 1967. Many EA-1Es were re-designated A-1G when they were transferred from the Navy into either the U.S. or Vietnamese Air Force. (Jim Sullivan Collection)

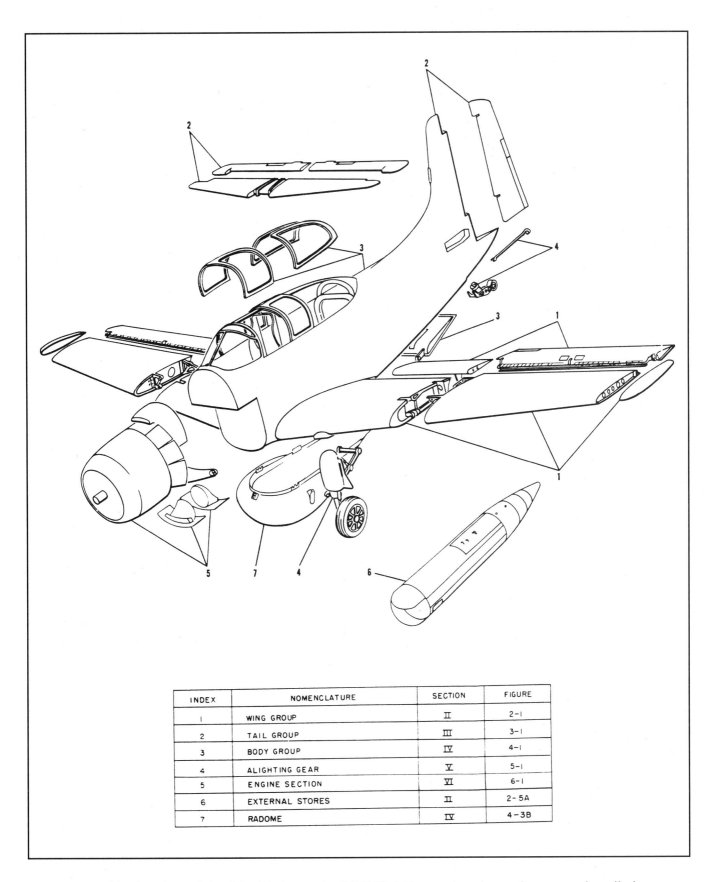

INDEX	NOMENCLATURE	SECTION	FIGURE
1	WING GROUP	II	2-1
2	TAIL GROUP	III	3-1
3	BODY GROUP	IV	4-1
4	ALIGHTING GEAR	V	5-1
5	ENGINE SECTION	VI	6-1
6	EXTERNAL STORES	II	2-5A
7	RADOME	IV	4-3B

Major assembly drawing of the AD-5W shows the AN/APS-20B search radar pod, commonly called a guppy radome. Under the left wing is the Aero 3A external stores pod (#6), which held the AN/APT-16 ECM equipment, a searchlight, or a chaff dispenser. The AD-5 had only a single dive brake panel under the fuselage (#3). (Walt Fink)

This VAW-11 AD-5W has just caught the wire aboard USS Kearsarge during the SEATO operation Exercise Sea Lion in August 1960. The Sea Lion operations were held in the South China Sea at a location that four years later would be known to the world as Yankee Station. (U.S. Navy)

SANDYS AND SPADS: THE ANTIQUE AIR FORCE

The Air Force had been interested in the Skyraider as far back as the late 1940s. But the (then) brand-new U.S. Air Force wanted an all-new image—an all-jet image. Propeller aircraft were a holdover from the Army Air Force. However, combat in Korea soon revealed that the Air Force jets were a little too fast for the close air support mission. Experience, increased training and better tactics and equipment, all would later show that the Air Force jets could do the job, but during the Korean War, the Air Force had to resort to using the F-51D Mustang as its premier close air support aircraft. The Air Force would never admit it, but inter-service rivalry also played a significant part in the Air Force turning down the Navy attack plane.

Nine years after the end of the Korean War, Air Force officers were

In early 1964, the U.S. Air Force borrowed two Navy A-1Es to test their feasibility for the Counter-Insurgency (COIN) mission. The first aircraft assigned to the 1st Air Commando Wing at the Special Air Warfare Center at Eglin AFB, Florida, were identical to Navy aircraft except for the overall gray (F.S. 16473) paint. (U.S. Air Force)

In May 1964, the first Air Force A-1Es were deployed to South Vietnam as part of the Farm Gate detachment at Bien Hoa. Assigned to the 1st Fighter Squadron (Commando) in the 34th Tactical Group, the A-1Es flew their first mission one day after arriving in-country on June 1, 1964. An Air Force armorer is removing unexpended rounds from the M3 20MM guns in the de-arming pits at Bien Hoa. (USAF)

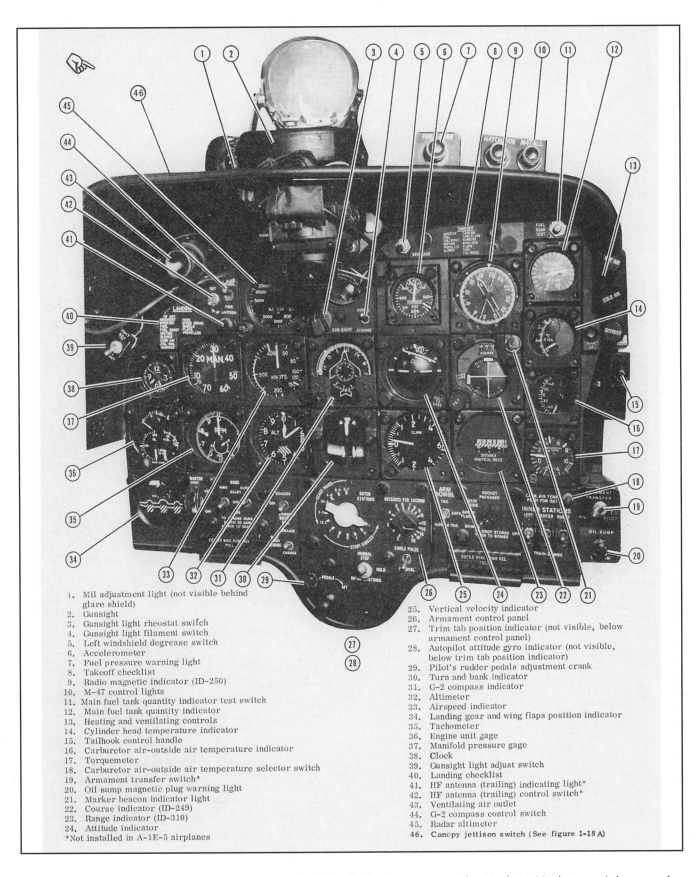

1. Mil adjustment light (not visible behind glare shield)
2. Gunsight
3. Gunsight light rheostat switch
4. Gunsight light filament switch
5. Left windshield degrease switch
6. Accelerometer
7. Fuel pressure warning light
8. Takeoff checklist
9. Radio magnetic indicator (ID-250)
10. M-47 control lights
11. Main fuel tank quantity indicator test switch
12. Main fuel tank quantity indicator
13. Heating and ventilating controls
14. Cylinder head temperature indicator
15. Tailhook control handle
16. Carburetor air-outside air temperature indicator
17. Torquemeter
18. Carburetor air-outside air temperature selector switch
19. Armament transfer switch*
20. Oil sump magnetic plug warning light
21. Marker beacon indicator light
22. Course indicator (ID-249)
23. Range indicator (ID-310)
24. Attitude indicator
*Not installed in A-1E-5 airplanes

25. Vertical velocity indicator
26. Armament control panel
27. Trim tab position indicator (not visible, below armament control panel)
28. Autopilot attitude gyro indicator (not visible, below trim tab position indicator)
29. Pilot's rudder pedals adjustment crank
30. Turn and bank indicator
31. G-2 compass indicator
32. Altimeter
33. Airspeed indicator
34. Landing gear and wing flaps position indicator
35. Tachometer
36. Engine unit gage
37. Manifold pressure gage
38. Clock
39. Gunsight light adjust switch
40. Landing checklist
41. HF antenna (trailing) indicating light*
42. HF antenna (trailing) control switch*
43. Ventilating air outlet
44. G-2 compass control switch
45. Radar altimeter
46. Canopy jettison switch (See figure 1-18 A)

The left main instrument panel of the A-1E had all the flight instruments. The Mark 20 Mod 4 gunsight was also located only on the left side of the cockpit, although the co-pilot could fire the guns and operate all the weapons systems. (Mac)

A 1st FS(C) A-1E taxis to the active runway at Bien Hoa in July 1965 carrying a full load of BLU-1 fire bombs for an anti-personnel strike in South Vietnam. USAF A-1Es were supposed to fly combat missions _only_ when a Vietnamese pilot was in the right seat. This rule was loosely enforced, and the VNAF pilot was actually any Vietnamese national who was nearby. (Staff Sergeant David Menard)

forced to begin flight operations in the old AD, which was so old that it was nicknamed the Spad. The U.S. State Department wanted to equip the fledgling Republic of Vietnam Air Force, the VNAF, with A-1 Skyraiders to fight the communist guerrillas who were attempting to overthrow the Diem government in South Vietnam. The Air Force would handle the training of Vietnamese Air Force (VNAF) pilots in the Skyraider, but first they had to be trained themselves. After all, almost no one in the Air Force knew anything about a tail-dragger pro-

peller-driven aircraft, let alone the Skyraider. The Air Force borrowed a pair of A-1Es from the Navy, tested the aircraft for use in the counter-insurgency (COIN) role, and made recommendations as to equipment needed to train other pilots.

For the training of both USAF and VNAF pilots, the Air Force A-1Es were modified with dual flight controls, plus Air Force radio and navigational equipment. A second throttle assembly was mounted on the center console, and a second set of rudder pedals was added to

the right cockpit. The right control stick was removable, and it was stowed on the right side of the cockpit when not in use.

The rear canopy of Air Force A-1Es was tinted a deep blue, which resulted in the rear cockpit area being called the Blue Room. Although the rear cockpit area was intended for personnel use by the Navy, in some of the Air Force A-1Es, two large fuel tanks were mounted in the Blue Room. Each of these tanks held 155 gallons of fuel, which more than made up for the

Seven A-1Es from the 1st FS(C) on the ramp at Qui Nhon in early 1965. Air Force A-1Es differed from Navy aircraft in having dual flight controls and Air Force radios and navigational equipment. Detachments of A-1Es operated from Forward Operating Locations, or FOLs, during the early months of U.S. involvement. 1st FS(C) aircraft carried large single digit numbers on their engine cowls as a squadron identifier. (Paul Lake)

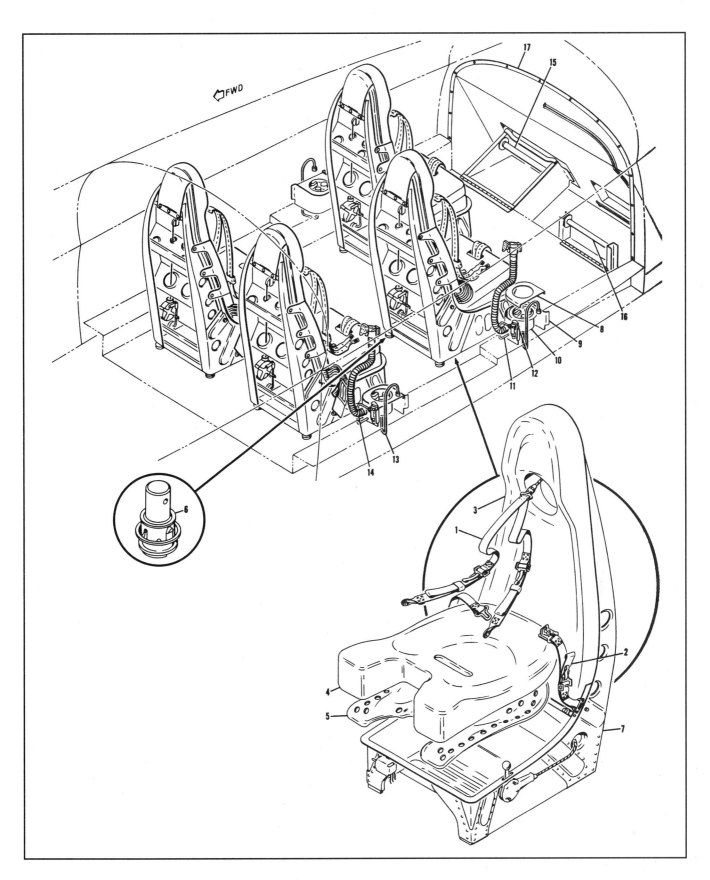

The multi-place AD-5 could be equipped with a variety of rear compartment kits, including a pair of four-seat conversions, an ambulance kit, and cargo hauling equipment that included an on-board hoist system. Each seat had its own oxygen regulator. (Walt Fink)

The second A-1E squadron operational in Vietnam was the 602nd FS(C), based at Pleiku in May 1964. This 602nd A-1E (52-132425) on the ramp at DaNang in January 1966 carries six LAU-3A rocket pods. The aircraft was lost over Laos on April 19, 1966. (USAF)

One of the missions pioneered by the 602nd (now) Air Commando Squadron was the search and rescue or SAR support mission, which was to escort rescue helicopters and suppress enemy fire around a downed pilot. Carolyn's Folly carries a single letter code on the engine cowling signifying a 602nd ACS aircraft. (USAF)

external fuel tanks that had been removed to make room for more ordnance. a 12.5-gallon additional oil tank sat in the aft compartment. Oil for the big R-3350 was something a Spad pilot never had enough of.

During the later half of 1966, A-1s were equipped with a poor man's ejector seat called the Yankee Extraction System, which was built by Stanley Aviation Corporation in Denver, Colorado. It was simple enough. On the A-1E/G, a rocket charge blew a canopy breaker tool through the canopy (the A-1H/J canopy was jettisonable), pulling the pilot upright in the cockpit. The seat automatically folded down as the rocket first pulled the pilot into an erect position, then pulled him through the canopy and free of the airplane. The rocket then deployed a pilot chute, which in turn, pulled the main chute. It worked quite well, even at zero altitude.

The mission of the Skyraider in USAF service would be that of a COIN aircraft, the same as the

During the early years of the war, Air Force A-1Es were painted an overall gray with a black anti-corrosion area immediately behind the exhausts. The extreme exhaust staining on this 1st ACS A-1E (52-133888) was normal. On March 13, 1968, this A-1E was shot down over Laos with the loss of both pilots. (via SSGT David Menard)

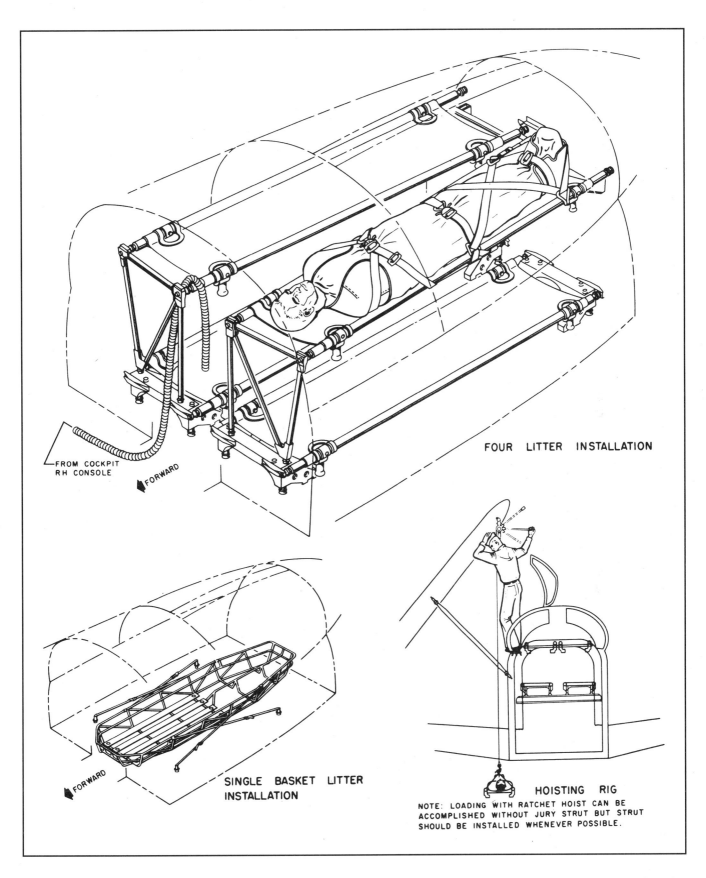

FOUR LITTER INSTALLATION

FROM COCKPIT
RH CONSOLE   FORWARD

FORWARD

SINGLE BASKET LITTER
INSTALLATION

HOISTING RIG

NOTE: LOADING WITH RATCHET HOIST CAN BE
ACCOMPLISHED WITHOUT JURY STRUT BUT STRUT
SHOULD BE INSTALLED WHENEVER POSSIBLE.

The multi-place AD-5 series could be equipped to carry litters and used as a flying ambulance. The kits modified the rear cockpit, so either a single Stokes basket or up to four standard litters could be carried. The litters were hoisted into the cockpit using the cargo hoist attached to the folded wingtip. (Mac)

The cockpit of the A-1E on display at the U.S. Air Force Museum shows the flight instruments and the Mk. 20 Mod 4 gunsight on the left side only, the dual-control columns, and the navigational equipment on the right side. The display aircraft, A-1E 52-132649, was flown by Medal of Honor recipient Major Bernie Fisher. (USAFM)

This 1st ACS A-1E carries an ordnance load typical of that found on a SAR mission: LAU-59 rocket pods and a 250-pound Willie Pete (white phosphorous) bomb under its left wing, SUU-11A/A mini-gun pod on the left pylon, and more LAU-59s and SUU-14 dispensers under its right wing. The asymmetrical drop tank configuration was normal when only one mini-gun was carried. (Tom Hansen)

VNAF's mission. For that mission, the A-1 was ideal with its ability to haul huge ordnance loads, plus its long loiter time over the target. In 1966, the crews of the 1st Air Commando Squadron experimented with a modified napalm tank, which they used to drop supplies to beleagured troops that otherwise could not be re-supplied. It worked, but a C-123 LABS drop was much better.

The dual-control A-1E was the aircraft used in South Vietnam, with a VNAF pilot in one seat and a USAF pilot in the other (supposedly). The Geneva Accords called for *(text continued on page 70)*

THE SKYRAIDER'S COLORS

FROM BLUE TO GRAY TO GREEN-AND-BROWN

The Douglas Skyraider has been flown in virtually every color scheme flown by armed forces since the end of World War Two. It was rolled out in natural metal, but all initial production aircraft were delivered in Glossy Sea Blue overall (F.S. 15042). In 1957, the Navy adopted a new tactical paint scheme, consisting of Gloss Gull Grey (F.S 16440), with a Gloss White underside. Navy and Marine aircraft were painted the same scheme. Codes were in White on blue airplanes, and black on the grey aircraft. Air Force aircraft were initially painted an overall Aircraft Grey (F.S. 16473), which was changed in 1965 to Dark Green (F.S. 34079), Olive Green (F.S. 34102), and Tan (F.S. 30219), with a Light Grey (F.S. 36622) underside.

A two letter code system, painted in white, was adopted in 1966, that reflected the squadron the A-1 was assigned to. Night operations aircraft had a black underside and code letters. Foreign users of the A-I painted their aircraft to reflect the mission or service assigned; i.e., Royal Navy AEW-1s were painted Dark Sea Grey, French A-1s were painted Silver the same as their F-47Ds, while Vietnamese Air Force A-1s were initially painted as delivered in US Navy scheme, then camouflaged as on US Air Force aircraft.

My Lois, a VMA-121 AD-2 on the ramp at Pyongtaek in 1952, is armed with 250-pound bombs and napalm. The AD-2 was delivered in standard Navy Gloss Sea Blue (FS 15042) overall, with the white code letters "AK" and a plane-in-squadron number on its cowl and upper right wing. (M. Derrickson)

Two AD-5Ns from VC-33 at one of the forward bases in Korea in 1953. Assigned to USS Leyte, VC-33 maintained a land-based detachment for close air support night missions. Under each left wing is the plane-in-squadron number, followed by "NAVY." The white wingtips and rudder trim are a squadron marking. (JEM Aviation Slide)

The most colorful Navy markings were seen on utility aircraft. Often used for target-towing, UA-1Es like this VA-35 aircraft (132555) had Seaplane Grey (FS 16081) fuselages, Yellow (FS 13538) wings, and International Orange (FS 12197) tail surfaces. (David Menard)

In 1966, the Navy experimented with camouflage on tactical aircraft involved in the Vietnam War. VA-115 painted their A-1Hs' Dark Green (FS 34079) and Olive Green (FS 34102), while retaining the white underside. The camouflage did not help hide the aircraft over land, and actually hindered the deck crews during night operations. (Dick Starinchak)

Some of the gaudiest Navy markings were found on land-based units, which did not have the paint corrosion problems associated with sea duty. This VAQ-33 EA-1E was based at NAF Norfolk, Virginia, in September 1968. (Ron Picciani)

In 1957, the Navy's tactical paint scheme was officially changed to Gloss Gull Grey (FS 16440) with Gloss White undersides. Early unit codes consisted of a single letter on the tail and upper right wing of each aircraft in black. This AD-6 was assigned to VA-196 in May 1956. (Harrison Rued)

This A-1H, flown by Colonel Sam Berman, CO of the 6th SOS, was painted with the tail colors of a World War One Spad at DaNang in March, 1970. Air Force A-1s were camouflaged in Greens and Tan, with a light Grey underside. Most had names, some had artwork; but none were as colorful as Spad Dad. (Bob McGarry)

Although personal markings on Navy and Marine aircraft were, in general, kept at a minimum due to maintenance requirements, mission tallies were usually kept. The missions on this VA-152 A-1H are small bomb markers—105 in all. The ace of spades was VA-152's symbol when the squadron flew from the USS Oriskany during the Vietnam War. (Mike Grove)

Glider Rider, a VA-165 A-1H aboard the USS Intrepid in August 1966, illustrates the normal personal markings allowed on a Navy aircraft—a name on the nose and 60 mission marks. (Walt Ohrlick)

The AEW-1s that the Royal Navy sold to Sweden were stripped of their radar equipment, painted overall Gloss Yellow, and used as target tugs at Bromma in August 1973. (Lars Soldeus)

Aircraft assigned to the 522nd Fighter Squadron, 83rd Special Operations Group, and commanded by Nguyen Cao Ky, had unusual brown and green camouflage with special unit badges on the fuselage and engine cowl. At this time, 1963 to '64, VNAF aircraft were normally not camouflaged. (Terry Love)

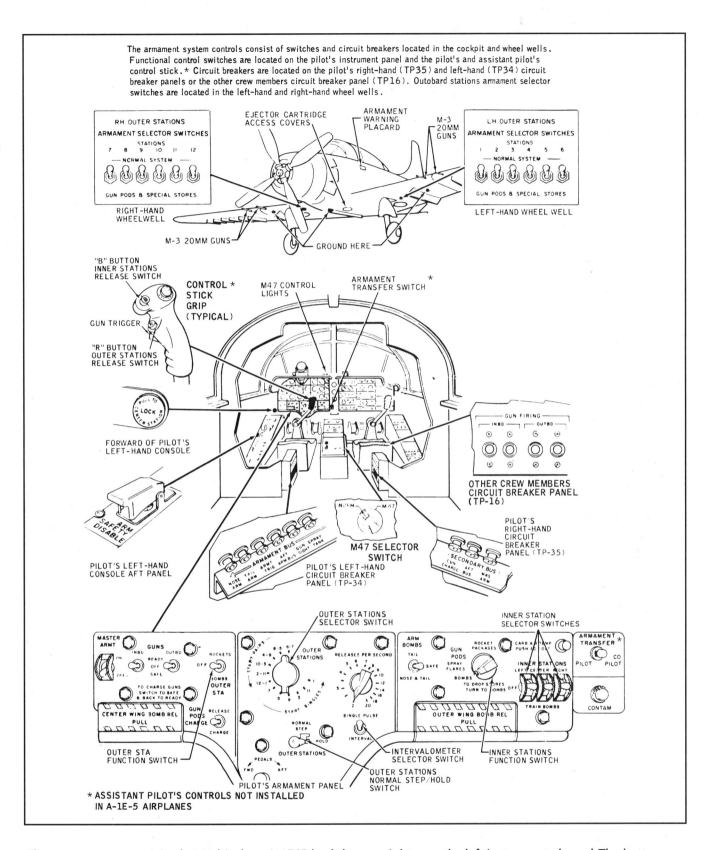

The armament system controls consist of switches and circuit breakers located in the cockpit and wheel wells. Functional control switches are located on the pilot's instrument panel and the pilot's and assistant pilot's control stick.* Circuit breakers are located on the pilot's right-hand (TP35) and left-hand (TP34) circuit breaker panels or the other crew members circuit breaker panel (TP16). Outobard stations armament selector switches are located in the left-hand and right-hand wheel wells.

RH OUTER STATIONS
ARMAMENT SELECTOR SWITCHES
STATIONS
7 8 9 10 11 12
NORMAL SYSTEM
GUN PODS & SPECIAL STORES

LH. OUTER STATIONS
ARMAMENT SELECTOR SWITCHES
STATIONS
1 2 3 4 5 6
NORMAL SYSTEM
GUN PODS & SPECIAL STORES

EJECTOR CARTRIDGE ACCESS COVERS
ARMAMENT WARNING PLACARD
M-3 20MM GUNS

RIGHT-HAND WHEELWELL
M-3 20MM GUNS
GROUND HERE
LEFT-HAND WHEEL WELL

"B" BUTTON INNER STATIONS RELEASE SWITCH
CONTROL* STICK GRIP (TYPICAL)
M47 CONTROL LIGHTS
ARMAMENT TRANSFER SWITCH *
GUN TRIGGER
"R" BUTTON OUTER STATIONS RELEASE SWITCH

PULL TO LOCK CENTER STATION
FORWARD OF PILOT'S LEFT-HAND CONSOLE

ARM SAFETY DISABLE
PILOT'S LEFT-HAND CONSOLE AFT PANEL

GUN FIRING
INBD   OUTBD
OTHER CREW MEMBERS CIRCUIT BREAKER PANEL (TP-16)

ARMAMENT BUS
NOSE TAIL ARMT AFT GUN SPRAY
TRIG ARM BUS RIGHT TANK
ARM

NORM — M47
M47 SELECTOR SWITCH
PILOT'S LEFT-HAND CIRCUIT BREAKER PANEL (TP-34)

PILOT'S RIGHT-HAND CIRCUIT BREAKER PANEL (TP-35)
SECONDARY BUS
GUN AFT MAS
CHARGE BUS ARM

OUTER STATIONS SELECTOR SWITCH
INNER STATION SELECTOR SWITCHES

MASTER ARMT
GUNS
INBD   OUTBD
READY
ON   OFF
OFF   SAFE
ROCKETS
OFF
BOMBS
OUTER STA
TO CHARGE GUNS SWITCH TO SAFE & BACK TO READY
GUN PODS CHARGE
RELEASE
CHARGE
CENTER WING 30MB REL PULL

START PAIRS
8-5 6-7
10-3
2-11
12-1
OUTER STATIONS
RELEASES PER SECOND
START SINGLES
SINGLE PULSE
NORMAL STEP
HOLD
INTERVAL
OUTER STATIONS
PEDALS
FWD   AFT

ARM BOMBS
TAIL
SAFE
NOSE & TAIL
GUN PODS SPRAY FLARES
ROCKET PACKAGES
CARB A&TEMP PUSH IN OUT
INNER STATIONS
LEFT CENTER RIGHT
BOMBS
OFF
TO DROP STORES TURN TO BOMBS
TRAIN BOMBS
OUTER WING BOMB REL PULL

ARMAMENT TRANSFER *
PILOT   CO PILOT
CONTAM

OUTER STA FUNCTION SWITCH
INTERVALOMETER SELECTOR SWITCH
INNER STATIONS FUNCTION SWITCH
PILOT'S ARMAMENT PANEL
OUTER STATIONS NORMAL STEP/HOLD SWITCH

* ASSISTANT PILOT'S CONTROLS NOT INSTALLED IN A-1E-5 AIRPLANES

The armament system in the multi-place A-1E/G had the gunsight over the left instrument shroud. The buttons on both control sticks released the weapons from the underwing stations, while the trigger on the front of both sticks fired either the M3 20MM cannon or the SUU-11A/B gatling gun. The Armament Control Panel under the instrument panel bore the Master Arm and gun charger switches, plus the intervalometer dial and rudder adjustment crank. (Mac)

An A-1E (52-132444) from the 602nd ACS catches the cable used to help stop battle-damaged aircraft at some of the FOLs in Laos and South Vietnam. The 633rd Consolidated Aircraft Maintenance Squadron at Pleiku was the primary A-1 maintenance facility in Vietnam. The large white serial number indicates that the change to tail codes is near. (USAF)

A 602nd ACS crew chief works on the engine accessories mounted behind the big R-3350 on the open ramp at DaNang in October 1966. Normal maintenance on the A-1s was performed on the open ramp wherever they were based. Note the different propeller tip markings: the Air Force used yellow, while the Navy had a red-white-red tip. The Playboy Bunny on the propeller was a unit marking. (Tom Hansen)

(text continued from page 64) a VNAF personnel to be aboard, but it did not necessarily have to be a pilot. In fact, there were times during the early days of the war when a VNAF sandbag was all that occupied the right seat. Department of Defense transferred 150 surplus A-1Es from the Navy to the Air Force in 1964. The serial numbers of Air Force A-1s simply reflected the original BuAer number, with the fiscal year the airplane was built added at the beginning, thus Navy A-1E Bu. No. 133918 built in 1952, became AF serial number 52-133918.

Initial training of USAF pilots, and tactics for the COIN mission, were developed at the Air Force Special Air Warfare Center, which was opened in April 1962 at Eglin AFB, Florida. On April 30, 1964, the first six Air Force A-1Es were ferried from Clark AB in the Philippines to the Special Air Warfare Center at

Camouflage paint colors of Dark Green (F.S. 34079), Olive Green (F.S. 34102), and Tan (F.S.30219), began to be applied to aircraft in 1965. Initially, no tail codes or other unit markings were used, just a serial number and a 15-inch national insignia on the fuselage only. This 602nd ACS A-1E (52-133867) was shot down over South Vietnam on March 10, 1966. (USAF)

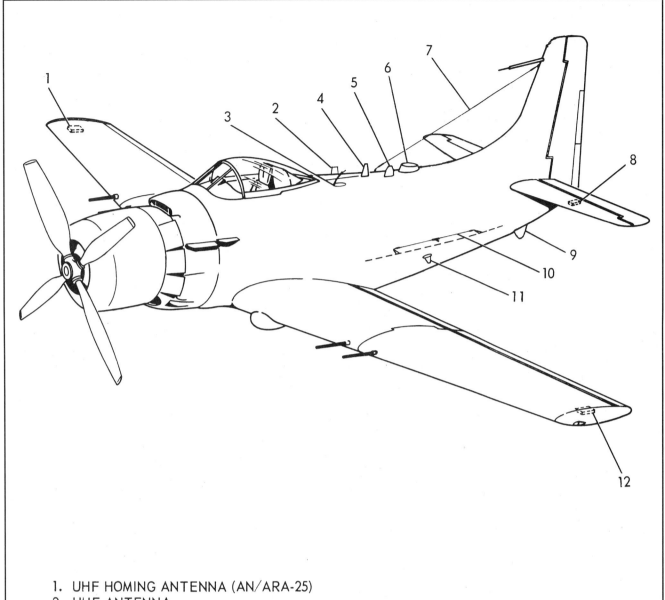

1. UHF HOMING ANTENNA (AN/ARA-25)
2. UHF ANTENNA
3. FM 622 ANTENNA
4. VHF/UHF RADIO (AN/ARC-27, AN/ARC-1)
5. TACAN (AN/ARN-21)
6. RADIO COMPASS LOOP (AN/ARN-6)
7. RADIO COMPASS SENSING (AN/ARN-6)
8. RADIO ALTIMETER (AN/APN-22)
9. FM HOMING
10. VHF-FM RADIO (AN/ARC-44)
11. IFF (AN/APX-6)
12. MARKER BEACON (AN/ARN-12)

Air Force and VNAF antenna configurations were quite different from the Navy aircraft, even though they operated in the same environment. The different antennaes included the FM 622 whip antenna used to establish contact with ground troops and the AN/ARC-27 (or ARC-1) UHF/VHF radio antenna, plus the AN/ARC-44 VHF/FM antenna under the fuselage. (Mac)

An A-1E from the 602nd ACS in 1965 has a full load of unfinned BLU-1 fire bombs. At this time, the 602nd was assigned to the 6251st TFW. This aircraft has a conglomerate of markings—a Navy tactical scheme in gray and white, with the Air Force miniature 15-inch insignia and serial used on camouflaged aircraft, painted over the original Navy markings. (JEM Aviation Slide)

Bien Hoa AB, Republic of Vietnam as part of Operation FARM GATE. The Skyraiders were assigned to the 1st Fighter Squadron (Commando), as part of the 34th Tactical Group, the parent unit in the FARM GATE operation. They flew their first mission the following day, June 1, 1964. Their initial mission was on-the-job (OJT) training of the Vietnamese Air Force, and support of Allied troops in combat situations in South Vietnam.

The A-1Es flew combat missions ostensibly as part of the OJT. Usually, the USAF pilots took the controls during the actual attack phase of the mission, especially when friendly troops were in the area. As VNAF pilots graduated, they were sent to VNAF squadrons of single-seat A-1Hs based throughout South Vietnam. It was in fact, one of these OJT flights that took the life of Colonel Thomas Hergert. Colonel Hergert was deputy chief of the Air Force section of the Military Assistance Advisory Group in South Vietnam. On March 8, 1964, Colonel Hergert was flying wing on a Vietnamese Air Force A-1 air strike against some Viet Cong positions near Saigon, when his aircraft suffered a .50-caliber hit and crashed.

On March 8, 1966, the 1st ACS was put under operational control of the 14th Air Commando Wing at Nha Trang. Tail codes began appearing in 1966, with "EC" assigned to the 1st ACS. The sign under the canopy reads "DANGER— SEATS ARE ARMED!" indicating that this A-1E has had the Yankee Extractor system installed. (Jim Sullivan Collection)

WARBIRD**TECH**
S E R I E S

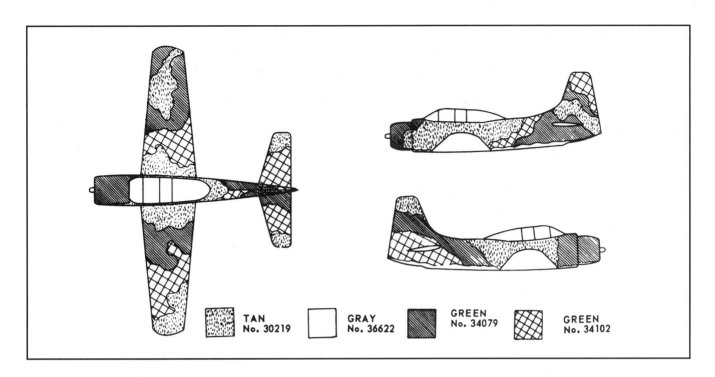

TAN No. 30219   GRAY No. 36622   GREEN No. 34079   GREEN No. 34102

Both U.S. Air Force and VNAF aircraft were camouflaged, beginning in 1965, using the same basic pattern. The upper colors were the same for USAF and VNAF, but the undersides of some USAF A-1s were painted black beginning in 1969. (Mick Roth)

24"

1/2 HEIGHT OF SERIAL NO.

2/3 HEIGHT OF SERIAL NO.

DISTINCTIVE UNIT AND SERIAL NUMBER SIZES A-1 AIRCRAFT

AF 33 715

15"

Tail codes were applied to U.S. Air Force aircraft beginning in 1966. Specifications called for the color of the tail codes to be Light Grey (F.S. 36622), but they were usually painted white on daylight operations aircraft (i.e. with the 36622 Grey undersides), and black on night operations aircraft. (Mick Roth)

An A-1E from the 1st ACS, 14th ACW at Nha Trang in 1967, is armed with LAU-3A rocket pods for an anti-personnel strike. The aircraft still has the Douglas factory-installed spoked main wheels as delivered to the Navy. (USAFM)

The 602nd ACS moved from Nha Trang to Udorn in April 1967 and was placed under operational control of the 432d Tactical Reconnaissance Wing. Flying the SANDY rescue mission, the 602nd also had a detachment on alert at Nakhon Phanom, the closest base to North Vietnam. (Tom Hansen)

Even after the training mission wound down, the USAF A-1Es remained in South Vietnam. For by that time, U.S. forces were heavily committed to combat, including many squadrons of USAF and Navy and Marine aircraft. At first, the Air Force A-1Es flew only troops-in-contact missions throughout all of South Vietnam.

Typical of the support mission, but one that turned out to be more than memorable, was the March 10, 1966, mission flown by Major Bernard Fisher, who was assigned to the 1st Air Commando Squadron at Pleiku. Hobo Flight was made up of six A-1Es loaded with bombs for anti-personnel strikes. They were to support some Special Forces GIs who were under attack at their base camp in the A Shau valley, about 150 miles from Pleiku. The North Vietnamese (NVA) wanted the base camp and had more than 2,000 troops in place for the attack.

The A Shau valley is less than a mile wide and about six miles long. There are mountains on one end and the country of Laos on the other (not that that mattered). It was called The Tube. The NVA had a lot of anti-aircraft weapons in place

This 1st ACS A-1E crashed at Nha Trang in 1968 and was then moved to the back of the runway, where it was stripped of every usable part. One of the things that hampered A-1 operations throughout the war was a lack of spare parts. (Doug Sloviak)

WARBIRD**TECH**
SERIES

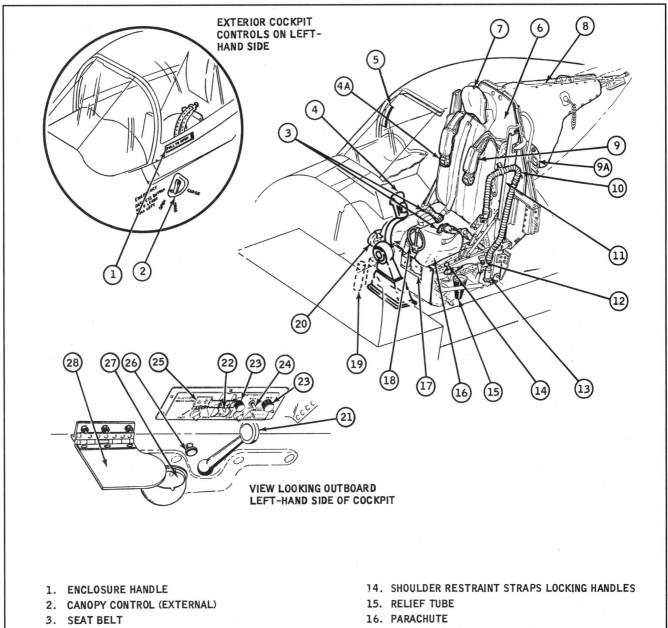

EXTERIOR COCKPIT
CONTROLS ON LEFT-
HAND SIDE

VIEW LOOKING OUTBOARD
LEFT-HAND SIDE OF COCKPIT

1. ENCLOSURE HANDLE	14. SHOULDER RESTRAINT STRAPS LOCKING HANDLES
2. CANOPY CONTROL (EXTERNAL)	15. RELIEF TUBE
3. SEAT BELT	16. PARACHUTE
4. CONTROL STICK	17. EXTRACTION CONTROL ASSEMBLY
4A. PARACHUTE CANOPY RELEASE FITTING (KOCH)	18. PRIMARY EXTRACTION FIRING CONTROL HANDLE
5. REAR VIEW MIRRORS (2)_LH/RH	19. NIGHT DRIFT SIGNALS
6. ARMOR PLATE	20. EMERGENCY HARNESS RELEASE HANDLE
7. HEAD REST	21. COCKPIT CANOPY CONTROL
8. EXTRACTION ROCKET STOWED	22. CANOPY JETTISON SWITCH
9. SHOULDER RESTRAINT STRAPS	23. CANOPY JETTISON TEST LIGHTS
9A. HYD. ENCLOSURE EMERGENCY AIR GAGE & FILLER VALVE	24. CANOPY JETTISON TEST SWITCH
10. OXYGEN BREATHING TUBE AND HEADSET CONNECTIONS	25. CANOPY JETTISON SWITCH GUARD
11. SEAT RAILS	26. CANOPY CONTROL RELEASE PLUNGER
12. ANTI-G DISCONNECT	27. ASH TRAY
13. PERSONNEL GEAR RECEPTACLE	28. ARM REST

The Stanley Aviation Co. designed an inexpensive but effective escape system for use in the A-1 during the mid-1960s. Known as the Yankee Extractor, the Stanley system pulled the pilot out of the cockpit rather than having the pilot physically leave the aircraft by climbing out onto the wing during bailout. Air Force aircraft (and some late Navy A-1Hs/Js) had the system installed as early as 1966. (Mac)

In 1968, Air Force began combat testing of the BLU-76/B Fuel Air Explosive (FAE) device. The 2,600-pound weapon used a volatile liquid as its explosive. On impact, the liquid rapidly mixed with air to form a highly unstable gas cloud, which was then detonated by a timed charge. The BLU-76/B FAE weapon on this 602nd SOS A-1E had the explosive power of 10,000-pounds of TNT! (via Tom Brewer)

on both sides of the valley, including heavy machine guns and 37mm automatic cannons. During Hobo Flight's first pass, the AAA put Captain Hubert King's A-1E out of action when a round went through his canopy, narrowly missing King. With his canopy missing, King limped back to Pleiku.

Major Fisher and two other Hobo A-1s raked both sides of the valley with bombs and 20mm cannon fire, as the A Shau Special Forces troops called out gun locations. Major D. Wayne Myers, "Jump" to his friends in the 602nd FS(C), started a run, but soon encountered several heavy caliber anti-aircraft guns, one of which knocked out the big R-3350 in Myers' A-1E. Jump had to make a quick decision whether to land on the crude air strip at A Shau. Retracting the landing gear, Myers ejected his aircraft's center-line drop tank just as his A-1E touched down on the PSP steel runway, and slid to a halt off the right side of the strip. The A-1E immediately burst into flames and Myers scrambled off the right wingtip into the scrub growth nearby.

Major Fisher and Captain "Paco" Vasquez watched as Myers made it to cover. Fisher took Hobo Flight down into the valley and began giving cover fire for Myers and the Special Forces troops. Fisher called the nearest command post, asking for a rescue chopper to pull out Myers. The controller replied that one was already en route, but it was 20 minutes out. Hobo Flight continued to strafe the NVA, trying to take out as many of the heavy AAA guns as possible. Ten minutes later Fisher again called the command post and asked where the chopper was. The controller replied that the chopper was still 20 minutes out, and he wanted Fisher to leave the area to guide the helicopter through the mist into A Shau. Major Fisher quickly vetoed that idea as he knew the NVA were closing in on his friend.

Fisher decided that he would try and make a pickup on the short A Shau strip to rescue Myers. Putting down his landing gear, Fisher began his approach. Vasquez was right on his wing strafing any NVA troops that stuck their heads out. Fisher put the big A-1E down on

A typical ordnance load for the search and rescue SANDY mission would include: (left to right) SUU-14 dispensers, 100-pound white phosphorous bomb, and various rocket pods. This 1st ACS A-1E also has the Mk. 8 300-gallon drop tanks. (Tom Hansen)

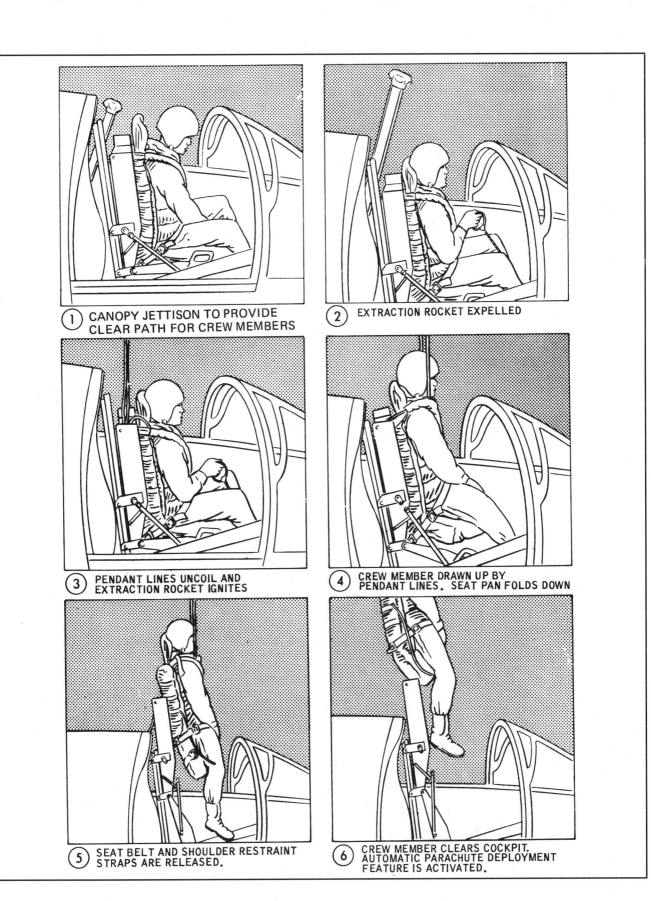

1. CANOPY JETTISON TO PROVIDE CLEAR PATH FOR CREW MEMBERS

2. EXTRACTION ROCKET EXPELLED

3. PENDANT LINES UNCOIL AND EXTRACTION ROCKET IGNITES

4. CREW MEMBER DRAWN UP BY PENDANT LINES. SEAT PAN FOLDS DOWN

5. SEAT BELT AND SHOULDER RESTRAINT STRAPS ARE RELEASED.

6. CREW MEMBER CLEARS COCKPIT. AUTOMATIC PARACHUTE DEPLOYMENT FEATURE IS ACTIVATED.

The Yankee Escape System first jettisoned the canopy, then fired a rocket through the opening which pulled the pilot erect and folded the seat down, finally pulling the pilot clear of the aircraft. Yankee Escape Systems were installed in both single-seat A-1H/Js and multi-place A-1E/Gs. (Mac)

War Monger, *an A-1E from the 6th SOS based at Pleiku, the third A-1 squadron operational in Vietnam. The 6th SOS flew close air support missions for the U.S. troops operating in South Vietnam, and was assigned to the 633rd SOW in 1968.* (Larry Sutherland)

the end of the 2,500-foot PSP steel runway. Dodging the debris and shell craters the entire length of the strip, Fisher tried to stop but couldn't. He poured the power back on and lifted off the metal air strip, made a 180-degree turn and started in from the opposite direction.

Putting his wheels down right on the edge of the steel matting, With the brakes smoking, Fisher again attempted to stop before he ran out of runway. Finally, in desperation, Fisher made a hard turn, sliding the big bird on the steel matting, rattled the tail off some steel drums in the weeds, and taxied back down the junk-strewn strip to

An indication of the immense size of both the A-1 and its Aeroproducts propeller is shown when compared with A1C Larry Sutherland, who is over 6 feet tall. The variable-pitch, constant-speed propeller has a 13-foot, 6-inch diameter. (Larry Sutherland)

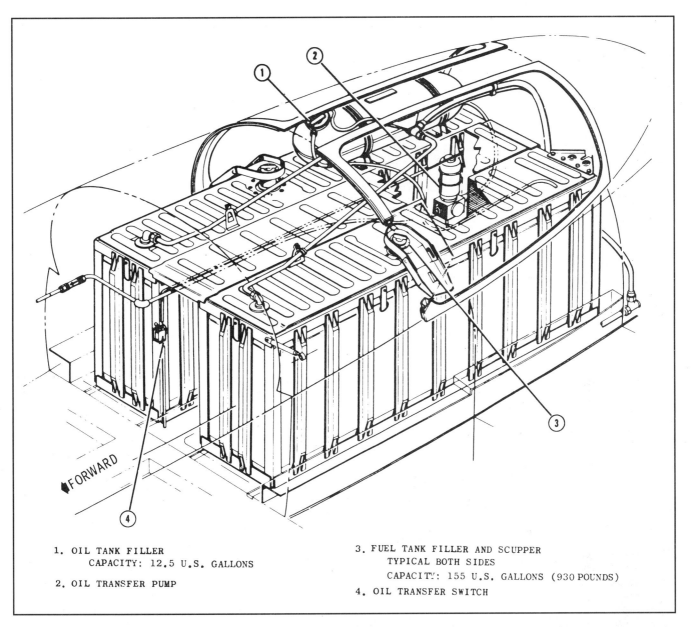

1. OIL TANK FILLER
   CAPACITY: 12.5 U.S. GALLONS

2. OIL TRANSFER PUMP

3. FUEL TANK FILLER AND SCUPPER
   TYPICAL BOTH SIDES
   CAPACITY: 155 U.S. GALLONS (930 POUNDS)

4. OIL TRANSFER SWITCH

(Above) Some very long flights called for additional fuel, and some AD-5/A-1E/Gs had an additional pair of 155-gallon fuel tanks installed in the rear cockpit area. An additional 12.5-gallon oil tank was also carried in the rear compartment. Oil was never a luxury for the A-1 driver. (Mac)

In April 1967, the 56th Air Commando Wing was established at Nakhon Phanom RTAB, commonly known as NKP or Naked Phanny. The 56th had both A-1 out-country units assigned, the 1st and 602nd ACS. The 1st ACS Hoboes, with the tail code "TC," flew interdiction missions against North Vietnamese traffic on the Ho Chi Minh Trail. (via Larry Davis)

The 602nd SOS flew the extremely hazardous SANDY missions—search and rescue into North Vietnam to retrieve downed U.S. pilots. This 602nd A-1H was hit by 37mm anti-aircraft fire and had to make a gear-up landing at Ubon in January 1969. Although badly damaged, the crews of the 633rd Combat Support Group at Pleiku will be able to put the aircraft back on flying status. (Al Piccirillo)

where Jump was anxiously waiting. His heart pumping, Fisher taxied the A-1 a little too fast and couldn't stop until he was a hundred feet past Myers. Myers sprinted to the idling Skyraider and jumped up on the wing. Fisher pulled him into the cockpit, flopping him down on the empty right seat floor.

As Paco and the other three Hobo A-1s made pass after pass over the NVA gunners, Fisher pushed the throttle forward, gingerly making his way in and around the junk and holes in the runway. At absolute minimum flying speed (the A-1E needed 103mph and 1,975 feet for takeoff), Fisher coaxed the big A-1E into the air, climbing out of A Shau valley just as another flight of A-1s arrived to take over the fight. Myers was a little the worse for wear, singed by the fire in his aircraft, but he was unharmed. Fisher's A-1E, #52-132649, had 19 holes in it. Thirteen of the 17 Special Forces troops were pulled out by helicopter, and the NVA took over what was left of the camp, which was promptly bombed by B-52 Arc Light strike. Major Bernard Fisher received the

Up close and personal with 1st Lieutenant R. Dorlund of the 1st SOS. Lieutenant Dortlund flew Blood, Sweat & Tears, *A-1H 52-139608. It's a view very reminiscent of World War I, flying open cockpit with the wind in your face.* (USAF)

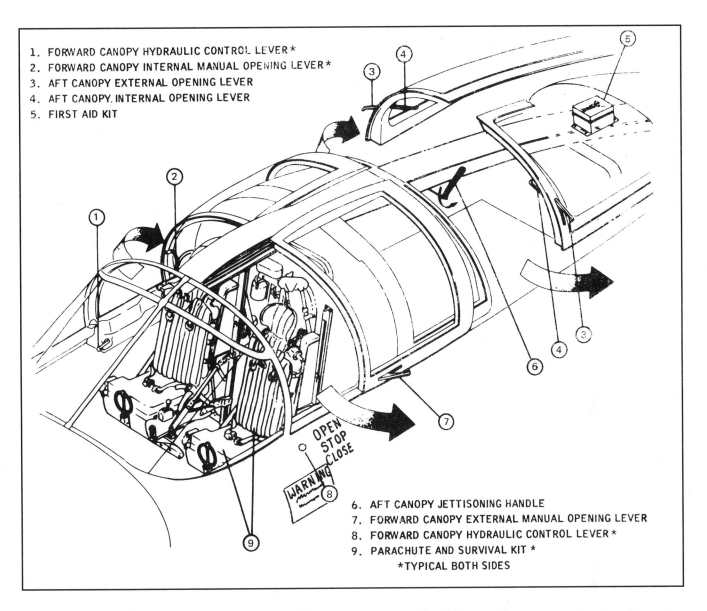

1. FORWARD CANOPY HYDRAULIC CONTROL LEVER *
2. FORWARD CANOPY INTERNAL MANUAL OPENING LEVER *
3. AFT CANOPY EXTERNAL OPENING LEVER
4. AFT CANOPY INTERNAL OPENING LEVER
5. FIRST AID KIT

OPEN
STOP
CLOSE

WARNING

6. AFT CANOPY JETTISONING HANDLE
7. FORWARD CANOPY EXTERNAL MANUAL OPENING LEVER
8. FORWARD CANOPY HYDRAULIC CONTROL LEVER *
9. PARACHUTE AND SURVIVAL KIT *
   *TYPICAL BOTH SIDES

An emergency exit from the multi-place AD-5 could be accomplished by sliding the front canopy back and opening the rear canopy hatches, then physically bailing out of the aircraft. Air Force aircraft in Vietnam had the Yankee Extractor System (shown), which ejected the crew from the front cockpit only. (Mac)

When the mission of the 1st SOS turned to night interdiction of The Trail, the crews repainted the undersides of their aircraft gloss black. Although repainted for the night interdiction mission, Blood, Sweat & Tears, a 1st SOS A-1H (52-139608), sits SAR alert at NKP in 1968. (Larry Davis)

Medal of Honor for his actions that day. His A-1E was rescued from a boneyard in Vietnam, restored, and now rests proudly in the U.S. Air Force Museum in Dayton, Ohio.

As the war expanded into other countries, so did the mission of the A-1. With Viet Cong supplies coming down the Ho Chi Minh Trail in a seemingly unending procession, the Air Force assigned the interdiction of traffic on The Trail to the 14th Air Commando Wing at Nha Trang. The 14th ACW was soon nick-named the Antique Air Force, as they flew nothing but old, some

very old, propeller aircraft in a supersonic Air Force. The pilots had already nick-named the Skyraider Spad, often flying the aircraft with the canopy open and scarves blowing in the prop wash.

The A-1 was a tough old bird, often coming home with large holes from accurate anti-aircraft fire. One example of the A-1's toughness occurred on a "Stretch" Ballmes mission. Stretch had just begun a run-in for a strafing attack, when the right 20MM cannon bay exploded. It was never discerned whether a communist shell had hit the guns

or not. The A-1G shuddered with the explosion but kept on flying. Ballmes, flying from the left seat of the A-1G, could not see the damage or the extent of the fire in the right wing. Upon landing at DaNang, he got out of the airplane and walked away as the crash crew put out the fire. Once the fire was out, Stretch returned to the airplane to survey the damage. The fire had burnt the skin off two-thirds of the wing inboard of the 20MM cannons. And it still flew! The ground crews at DaNang replaced the inner wing panel and the big A-1G was back in service.

The 14th ACW had squadrons and detachments (DETs) at bases and forward operating locations (FOLs) throughout South Vietnam. Several squadrons were based at Nakhon Phanom (NKP) Royal Thai Air Base on the extreme eastern tip of Thailand and at Udorn. The squadrons based at NKP were assigned to various units, including the 56th Air Commando Wing, and the 432nd Tactical Reconnaissance Wing was

Dimensions:

    Diameter — 30 inches

    Fin Span — 42 inches with standard fins

    Length — 167 inches

    Total Weight — 2600 pounds.

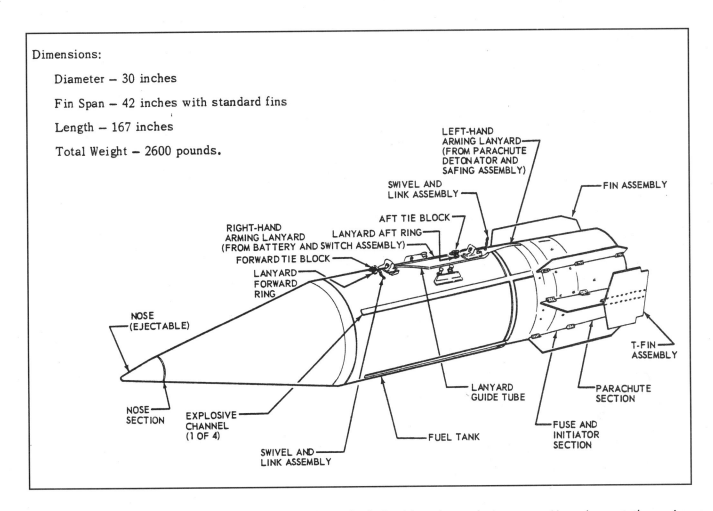

The BLU-76/B Fuel Air Explosive bomb used a highly volatile liquid as the explosive agent. Upon impact, the casing burst and the explosive liquid rapidly combined with the air, creating a highly explosive gas cloud. The gas cloud was ignited by a timed fuse, using 0.03-second delay timers to maximize the size of the gas cloud. The BLU-76/B was carried by A-1Es and was deployed using a parachute to retard the drop speed so that the delivery aircraft could get out of range. (Mick Roth)

Detachments of A-1s sat SAR alert at forward operating locations as near to North Vietnam as possible. Tiny Tim, a 602nd SOS A-1J (52-142056), sits cocked and ready in the SAR alert revetment at DaNang in May 1970, armed with CBU dispensers, rocket pods, Willy Pete bombs, and two SUU-11A/A gatling guns. (Lieutenant Colonel Barry Miller)

An A-1H (52-139803) from the 1st SOS with an unusual ordnance load: CBU-14 cluster bomb dispensers and Navy 5-inch LAU-10A Zuni rocket pods. All Air Force A-1s had a 1952 serial prefix, thus Navy A-1H BuAer 139803 became Air Force 52-139803. (B. Morrison)

the parent unit at Udorn. The primary A-1 maintenance unit was the 633rd Consolidated Aircraft Maintenance Squadron at Pleiku. The 633rd was designated a Special Operations Wing, with one A-1 squadron, the 6th SOS, being assigned in July 1968.

From NKP, the A-1s flew missions throughout Cambodia and Laos in support of U.S. advisor-led troops that were fighting the communist rebels in both countries. Operations over the Plaines des Jarres (PDJ) were known as Operation Barrel Roll, those in southern Laos were Operation Steel Tiger. The Antique Air Force of Douglas B-26Ks, A-1s, and North American T-28Ds had colorful call signs like Hobo, Firefly, Nimrod, and Zorro.

As the war widened in North Vietnam, a large number of USAF and Navy aircraft were shot down by North Vietnamese anti-aircraft and surface-to-air missiles. It was the most sophisticated air defense sys-

(left) Colonel Ed Walsh receives the ceremonial 100 mission bath as he exits his A-1H The Proud American at Nakhon Phanom in July 1971. (right) Colonel Walsh, CO of the 56th since August 1970, takes a big gulp of champagne prior to the 100 mission ride back to the NKP Officers Club. The logo on the fuselage reads "Colonel Walsh, #1 BOSS—c/c Sergeant Clark." (Frank Murray)

WARBIRDTECH
SERIES

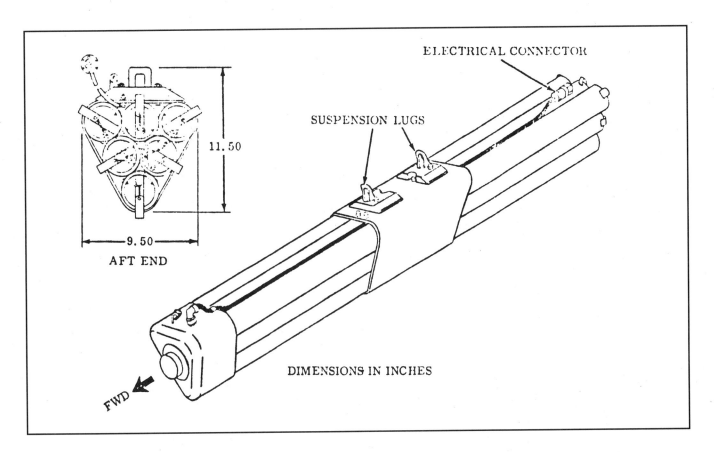

ELECTRICAL CONNECTOR

SUSPENSION LUGS

11.50

9.50

AFT END

DIMENSIONS IN INCHES

FWD

One of the main weapons used for the SANDY mission was the SUU-14A/A dispenser tubes, which could carry a large variety of different cluster bomb units. One of the more common CBUs was known as gravel, *a mud-like, jellied explosive that looked like small gravel or animal droppings when it dried on the ground, but it could take a man's foot off if stepped on.* (Mick Roth)

tem in the history of air warfare. The mission of the Skyraider pilots became to support the rescue of downed U.S. airmen inside North Vietnam or in any other country.

This mission made the A-1 a legend in Air Force annals. Operating in flights of four, call sign SANDY, their mission was to escort and support the rescue helicopters. It was not uncommon for the A-1 SANDYs to penetrate deep into the midst of "the most sophisticated air defense in history," including several missions well beyond Hanoi. And they did it with the slowest, least-sophisticated airplane in the Air Force inventory.

Flying low and slow, escorting the HH-3 Jolly Green Giant helicopters,

It's a well-known fact that if the centerline tank on an A-1 is not covered with oil, the pilot will refuse to fly the airplane! No matter how good the big R-3350 was maintained, it leaked oil. On this 602nd SOS A-1H, the nose flaps inside the engine cowl are fixed open. The heavy exhaust smoke as the engine starts was normal. (Robert F. Dorr)

The boneyard at Pleiku, home of the 633rd CAMS, was full of gutted A-1E hulks in 1968. Stripped of all usable pieces, this 1st ACS A-1G (52-134997) had been shot down over South Vietnam on November 22, 1966. The pilot was rescued and the A-1 was choppered back to Pleiku by a CH-54 Skycrane. (Larry Sutherland)

the SANDYs were armed with special weapons developed for the mission of Search and Rescue (SAR). SANDY A-1s carried at least one SUU-11A/B gatling gun pod under the wing, which was capable of spitting 6,000 7.62MM bullets per minute. Often the A-1s carried two SUU-11 pods, each with 1,500 rounds. They also had SUU-14 cluster bomb dispensers, which spread a jellied explosive called Gravel over a large area. As the Gravel dried out, it looked like rocks or animal manure and became active. When stepped on, however, it could take a man's foot off. The SANDYs also carried pods of rockets, napalm, and various bombs, as did the other A-1s flying against The Trail.

The SANDY mission was certainly one of the most dangerous in the Vietnam War, flying low and slow against the North Vietnamese air defense network of radar-directed AAA, SAMs, and MiGs. One of the SANDY missions resulted in a second Medal of Honor for an A-1 pilot. On September 1, 1968, Lieutenant Colonel William A. Jones was flying his 98th mission. Jones was SANDY 1, leading a flight of A-1s supporting a Jolly Green Giant that was attempting to rescue an F-4 pilot down in North Vietnam.

The F-4 pilot had gone down in the jungle northwest of Dong Hoi. After about an hour's delay, an F-100 pilot located the downed F-4 pilot and called Jones' flight to inform them of his position. The pilot was smack in the middle of a North Vietnamese flak trap, a nest of 37MM radar-directed automatic cannons. Arriving in the area, Jones broke down toward the jungle, trying to locate the downed flier. The NVA had guns in the hills on both sides of the downed F-4 pilot.

As the rest of SANDY Flight called out the locations of the AAA, the NVA gunners were starting to get the range on Jones' aircraft. One shell exploded so close to Jones A-1 that smoke from the explosion was pulled into Jones' cockpit. Lieutenant Colonel Jones continued to make passes, straining his eyes looking for the downed flier. Suddenly, the emergency radio squawked "An A-1 just passed over me!" Jones marked his map and began dropping ordnance on the NVA gun crews. Coming around for a second run, Jones' A-1H was raked with 14.5MM fire, and one of the rounds hit the rocket extractor

A detachment of 6th SOS A-1s was sent to Qui Nhon in 1969, and the tail codes modified from "ET" to "6T." Bad News sits five-minute alert armed with SUU-30 CBUs and Mk. 82 LDGP bombs with 36-inch "daisy cutter" fuse extenders. (Marty Isham)

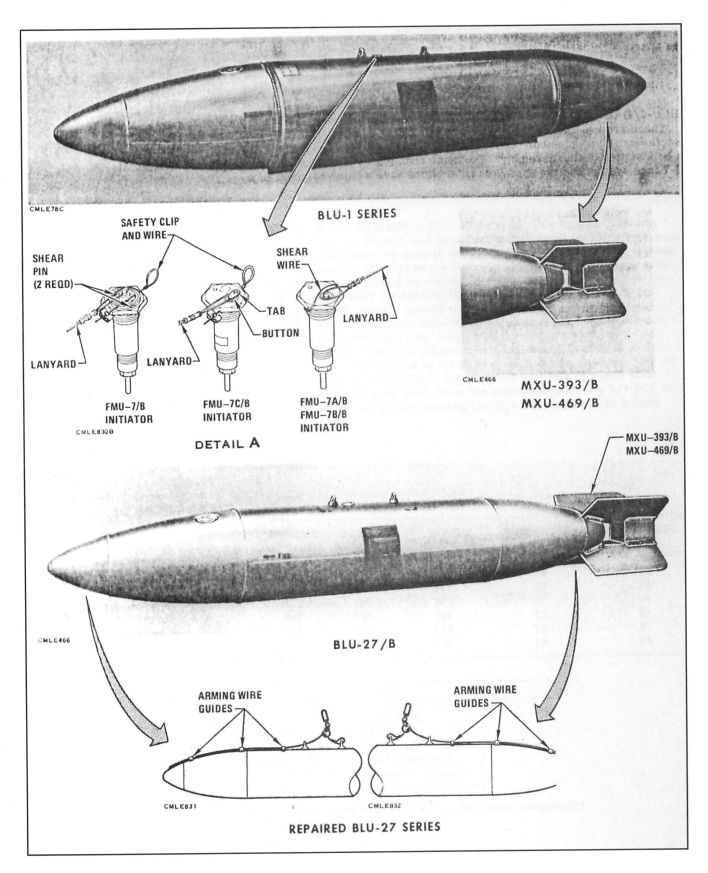

CMLE78C

BLU-1 SERIES

DETAIL A

SHEAR PIN (2 REQD)

SAFETY CLIP AND WIRE

SHEAR WIRE

LANYARD

TAB

BUTTON

LANYARD

LANYARD

FMU-7/B INITIATOR

FMU-7C/B INITIATOR

FMU-7A/B FMU-7B/B INITIATOR

CMLE830B

CMLE466

MXU-393/B
MXU-469/B

MXU-393/B
MXU-469/B

CMLE466

BLU-27/B

ARMING WIRE GUIDES

ARMING WIRE GUIDES

CMLE831

CMLE832

REPAIRED BLU-27 SERIES

Fire bombs were filled with a variety of flammable liquids, including jellied gasoline commonly known as napalm. The 700-pound BLU-1 series could be equipped with or without a stabilizing fin structure on the aft end of the bomb. A-1s in Vietnam carried up to five fire bombs under each wing. (Mick Roth)

The 6th SOS armament crews re-arm Honey with Mk. 82 500-pound LDGPs, using an MJ-1 bomb loader tractor in the revetment at Pleiku in 1968. The fuse extenders, up to 6 feet in length, will be screwed into the nose of each bomb after the weapon is attached to the wing pylon. (Larry Sutherland)

William Jones was awarded the Medal of Honor for his actions that day. The F-4 pilot was rescued later that day.

in his Yankee Extractor System seat. The rocket began to burn fiercely, but the seat did not activate and the rocket just burned hotly behind Jones.

Leaving the area, Jones tried to eject, but the Yankee system was inoperative. The canopy did jettison, which cleared the cockpit of smoke, but caused the rocket to burn even hotter in the fresh air. Jones called Hobo Flight to inform them he was bailing out and exactly where the F-4 pilot was located. Between all the radio traffic from his flight telling Jones to get out of the burning aircraft, and the damaged radio in the aircraft, Jones couldn't get through to anyone.

Jones decided to try to get back to

Nakhon Phanom with his information—and himself. If he bailed out, it would call for still another rescue attempt. NKP was over 90 miles away, and Jones was burned from the rocket over the entire upper third of his body. Captain Paul Meeks, SANDY 2, joined on his wing and talked his leader home. Jones put the A-1H down hard on the NKP runway, skidded to a stop, and waited for the crash trucks to arrive. As the firemen pulled him from his burnt out cockpit, Jones reached back in and grabbed his charts. He began telling the senior medics where the downed F-4 pilot was located, and the positions of the NVA AA guns. He was still giving information as he was strapped down on the operating table in the NKP hospital. Lieutenant Colonel

As the mission developed, the Air Force decided they needed another combat wing just for the out-country missions, such as trail interdiction and SAR missions into North Vietnam. In March 1967, the 56th Air Commando Wing (ACW), whose ancestry is traced back to Zemke's Wolfpack in World War Two, was established at NKP, taking over the squadrons already in place. All the A-1 missions into Laos, Cambodia, and North Vietnam were flown by 56th ACW squadrons. All air commando units were re-designated special operations units on August 1, 1968, thus the 56th ACW became the 56th Special Operations Wing. A third A-1-equipped wing, the 633rd Special Operations Wing, was activated in 1968 at Pleiku AB in South Vietnam.

With the war winding down and Vietnamization underway, the Air Force reduced the number of A-1

Miss Noreen, an A-1H from the 22nd SOS in one of the five-minute alert revetments at DaNang in 1971. The 22nd SOS was the fourth A-1-equipped squadron in the 56th SOW. The aircraft has four tan stripes on the rear fuselage, indicating a squadron commander's aircraft. (USAF)

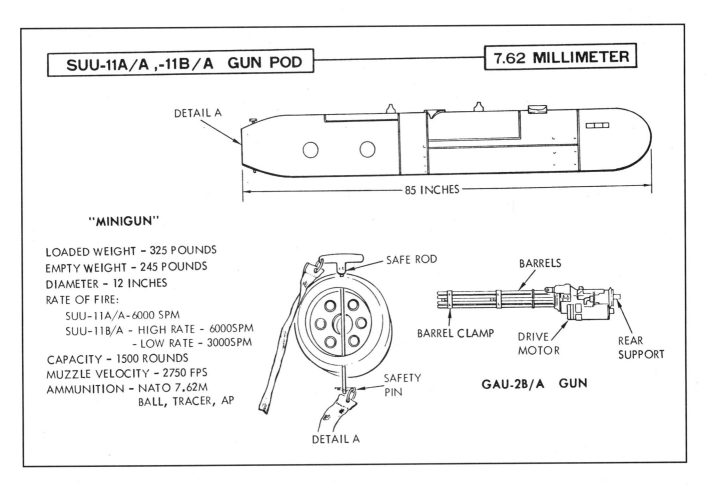

SUU-11A/A ,-11B/A GUN POD — 7.62 MILLIMETER

DETAIL A

85 INCHES

"MINIGUN"

LOADED WEIGHT - 325 POUNDS
EMPTY WEIGHT - 245 POUNDS
DIAMETER - 12 INCHES
RATE OF FIRE:
SUU-11A/A-6000 SPM
SUU-11B/A - HIGH RATE - 6000SPM
- LOW RATE - 3000SPM
CAPACITY - 1500 ROUNDS
MUZZLE VELOCITY - 2750 FPS
AMMUNITION - NATO 7.62M
BALL, TRACER, AP

SAFE ROD

SAFETY PIN

DETAIL A

BARRELS

BARREL CLAMP

DRIVE MOTOR

REAR SUPPORT

GAU-2B/A   GUN

The primary weapon of the Air Force Search and Rescue teams, the SANDYs, was the SUU-11A/B gatling gun pod, which contained a GAU-2B electrically driven 7-62MM gatling gun that fired at a rate of either 3,000 or 6,000 rounds per minute. Each pod held 1,500 rounds. The SUU-11A/B pods were carried on the Mk. 51 wing pylons. (Larry Davis)

squadrons in Southeast Asia. Most of the A-1s were transferred to the VNAF. By 1971, only the 1st SOS was still operating the A-1. DETs of 1st SOS A-1 SANDYs were still on alert at FOLs such as DaNang (Operating Location Alpha Alpha), and for search and rescue missions into southern and eastern North Vietnam. And the main portions of the squadron were still flying interdiction and SAR missions from NKP.

Even though the North Vietnamese air defenses became more intense as the war dragged on, the SAR teams of Jolly Greens and SANDYs continued to successfully rescue downed U.S. airmen almost until the end of the air war over the North. The last Air Force A-1 SANDY

Late in the war, the search and rescue team was comprised of a pair of HH-53 Super Jolly Green Giants and four A-1 SANDYs. Two of the SANDYs flew ahead of the choppers to attempt to pinpoint the downed pilot's location. The second pair of A-1s escorted the HH-53s to the area. The HH-53 could be refueled in-flight from an HC-130 tanker. (Don Jay)

Magnet Ass, *a 1st SOS SANDY sitting SAR alert at DaNang in May 1970 is armed with CBU dispensers, finned napalm and dual gatling gun pods. Magnet Ass, named by the pilot due to its ability to attract anti-aircraft gun fire, has a brand new tire on the right wheel.* (Lieutenant Colonel Barry Miller)

An A-1E (52-135141) flown by the CO of the 1st SOS at NKP in 1970. Commanders had multiple stripes painted on their aircraft in tan (F.S. 30219), four stripes for a squadron CO, five for a wing commander. This A-1E was one of three A-1s downed by SA-7 Strella missiles on May 2, 1971, effectively ending the A-1 involvement in the Vietnam War. (Petty via Menard)

Cool Fool, A-1H 52-134551, was assigned to Captain C. Miller in the 1st SOS in 1971, is re-armed and refueled at NKP. A 1st SOS armorer is reloading the M3 20mm cannons in the wing. The Fool was another A-1 lost to SA-7 Strella missiles on May 2, 1971. (via Larry Davis)

mission was flown by a 1st SOS A-1H on November 7, 1972. Two months later, the air war over North Vietnam was over.

By the end of the A-1 war in Southeast Asia, the Air Force had lost 197 A-1s, 159 of those were combat losses. The total included 112 of the original 150 A-1Es that had been transferred from the Navy. This total does not include VNAF aircraft lost in combat, of which there were many.

Although the SPAD was a tough old bird, it was certainly outclassed by the radar-directed air defenses put up by the communists. The end of the combat career of the A-1 was imminent when three Air Force A-1s and one VNAF A-1, were shot down by shoulder-fired SA-7 Strella heat-seeking missiles over South Vietnam on May 1 and 2, 1972. The SAR mission during the Linebacker II operation was flown by Air Force A-7D Corsair II jets.

The A-7s could never live up to the legend of the Spads and their crews. By the end of the war in Southeast Asia, 13 A-1 pilots had been awarded the Air Force Cross, and two had received the Medal of Honor. The old Spad had proven herself in both post-World War Two conflicts and been acclaimed by all who flew her.

SKYRAIDERS IN FOREIGN SERVICE

THE AEW I AND THE VNAF

Foreign use of the Skyraider was somewhat curtailed by the fact that Douglas Aircraft Company was hard-pressed to keep up the pace of deliveries to the U.S. Navy and Marine Corps. Douglas was also building A-4 Skyhawk jets at the same time that production of the Skyraider was peaking. The many variations that were possible using the Skyraider airframe, though, made the type appealing to a number of nations with special needs.

One of those nations was Great Britain, whose need was an airborne early warning aircraft for the Royal Navy. Douglas had one such model available and in production—the AD-4W. The AD-4W was a three-place aircraft that

housed the APS-20 scanning radar in a large, bulbous guppy radome under the fuselage. The Royal Navy purchased fifty AD-4Ws, 20 of which were new production aircraft (Bu. Nos. 127942 through 127963). The last 30 aircraft were drawn from surplus U.S. Navy inventories. The Royal Navy designated these aircraft as the Skyraider AEW I.

Only two Royal Navy squadrons were assigned Skyraider AEW I air-

craft: No. 778 Training Squadron and No. 849 Squadron. The first AEW Is were delivered to No. 778 Squadron at RNAS Culdrose in November 1951. Fleet operations with the No. 849 Squadron commenced when A Flight, 849 Squadron, began operations from the HMS Eagle on January 29, 1953. Each of the four Royal Navy aircraft carriers had a flight of four AEW Is assigned. The Royal Navy operated the AEW I for the next eight years, before replacing

In the early 1960s, the Royal Navy sold 12 AEW-1s to Sweden. The Swedish Air Force stripped the aircraft and converted them to target towing duties, painting them overall yellow. (L. Swenson)

The French Armie de l'Aire operated 93 AD-4s throughout the 1960s, flying combat against guerrilla forces in Algeria during the war of independence. This French AD-4N (125724) from Escadron 1/20 in Algeria is armed with T.10 rockets. French AD-4s underwent several modifications before going to combat units, including removal of the tail hook assembly and neutralization of the dive brakes. In November 1964, this aircraft was delivered to the Cambodian Air Force. (Jim Sullivan Collection)

A pair of AD-4Ns from E.A.A. 1/20 flew combat in Djibouti in 1963. These aircraft both have 150-gallon drop tanks and T.10 rockets. All French AD-4s had the four 20MM cannon. Several French AD-4s were still in flying condition in the early 1980s. (David Menard Collection)

One of the last French AD-4s in service was AD-4N 126877, which had been delivered on July 7, 1960. The aircraft flew combat in Algeria and Djibouti before it was withdrawn from service in December 1976. It was restored and displayed at Chateudun AFB in 1977. (Jim Sullivan Collection)

them with Fairey Gannet AEW aircraft. Included in that service was a short stint of combat during the 1956 Anglo-French intervention in the Middle East. After retiring the type in the early 1960s, 12 AEW Is were sold to Sweden, where they were stripped of their AEW systems, including the guppy radome, and used as target tugs.

In 1959, France became the second nation to be equipped with the Skyraider. Needing a fighter-bomber to replace their tired P-47D Thunderbolts, the Armie de l'Aire obtained 113 ex-U.S. Navy AD-4s from surplus stocks under the Military Assistance Plan. Twenty AD-4s, five AD-4NAs and 88 AD-4Ns were procured and rebuilt by SFERNA before entering service. All aircraft were taken to AD-4NA status, i.e. it was stripped of all night attack systems, the tail hook assembly was removed, the dive brake systems neutralized, and French radio and navigational equipment was installed, plus it had all the latest structural modifications as called for by the U.S. Navy and Douglas. The first French aircraft were deliv-

The first AD-6s were delivered to the Vietnamese Air Force, based at Bien Hoa AB near Saigon, in early September 1960. These A-1Hs were assigned to different flights within the VNAF 1st Fighter Squadron in September 1962, as denoted by the different colored fuselage bands. (USAF)

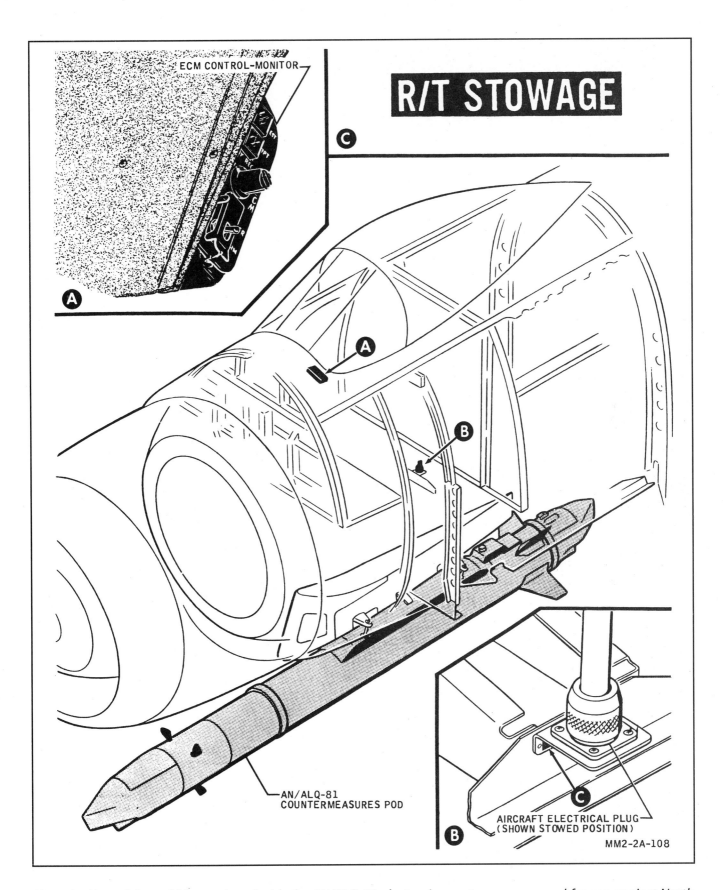

R/T STOWAGE

ECM CONTROL-MONITOR

A

B

C

AN/ALQ-81
COUNTERMEASURES POD

AIRCRAFT ELECTRICAL PLUG
(SHOWN STOWED POSITION)

MM2-2A-108

Navy A-1Hs and Js could be equipped with the AN/ALQ-81 electronic countermeasures pod for use against North Vietnamese AAA and SAM radars. Carried on the Aero 3A centerline rack, the ALQ-81 had their own electrical system using a ram air turbine in the forward part of the pod. (Mick Roth)

VNAF A-1Hs were delivered in the standard Navy paint scheme of Gull Grey (FS 36440) and white. This VNAF A-1H (135367) has a tiger insignia on its cowl, indicating an A-1 from the 2nd Fighter Squadron at DaNang in October 1964. (Staff Sergeant David Menard)

ered to the 20th Escadre in February 1960, equipping the first of three *escadrons* (squadrons). Escadrons I/20 and III/20 were committed to the conflict in Algeria against the Front de Liberation Nationale, where they flew counter-insurgency missions until 1963 when Algeria was granted independence.

French Skyraiders also flew combat against guerrillas operating in French Somaliland, Malagassy, and Chad, before finally being retired in the early 1970s. Many of the French Skyraiders were sold to the other nations that were involved in some of these brush-fire wars. In 1965, 15 of the French AD-4NAs were sold to the Kingdom of Cambodia, over the objections of the U.S. government. But Prince Sihanouk's government prevented their use against the Viet Cong and North Vietnamese that were operating against South Vietnam from bases inside Cambodia. Following the ouster of Sihanouk in 1970, the Cambodian Skyraiders did begin flying combat missions against the communists, but the effort was both feeble and short-

A VNAF 1st FS pilot (maybe!) taxiing for take-off from Bien Hoa in July 1965, carries a pair of M65 1,000-pound bombs and six 500-pound bombs. The VNAF had A-1s in service from September 1960 through the fall of South Vietnam in 1975. (Staff Sergeant David Menard)

A newly delivered VNAF A-1E taxis to the active runway at Nha Trang in November 1966 carrying eight BLU-1 napalm tanks. Assigned to the 516th FS, the aircraft is already flying combat missions, even before any markings have been applied— no insignias, not even a serial. (Terry Love)

WARBIRD**TECH**
SERIES

A VNAF 516th FS A-1E on its nose at Nha Trang in 1965. VNAF A-1Es were identical to USAF A-1Es, with dual flight controls, but without the tail hook assembly. The 516th FS converted from T-28Ds to A-1s in 1963. (David Menard Collection)

lived. In 1976, France turned over six of the AD-4NAs to the government of Chad for operations against the Libyan forces that were attempting to take over the country. Gabon also received four ex-French Skyraiders in the late 1970s. Both the Chad and Gabon aircraft were flown by ex-Armie de l'Aire pilots until as late as 1980.

By far, the most numerous amount of Skyraiders serving in non-U.S. forces were those operated by the Republic of Vietnam Air Force, or VNAF. The Eisenhower administration sent six Skyraiders to the VNAF in September 1960, with 25 more following in the spring of 1961. Sent to Saigon aboard *USS Cord*, a

The elite squadron in the Vietnamese Air Force was the 522d FS of the 83rd Special Operations Group, commanded by Nguyen Cao Ky, who later became vice president of the Republic of Vietnam. The 522nd FS A-1s had a distinctive red-brown and green camouflage, with special markings and insignia that represented the 83rd SOG dragon, and five stars for the manly virtues of Confucianism. (Terry Love)

As U.S. Air Force aircraft began adopting tactical camouflage in 1965, the VNAF aircraft were painted an identical scheme. These 516th FS A-1Hs have the blue band with white stars representing the 41st Tactical Wing, based at DaNang in 1966, with no national insignia at this time. (Tom Hansen)

converted U.S. Navy jeep carrier, the A-1Hs were unloaded and towed to Tan Son Nhut AB. The training of VNAF air crews began at Randolph AFB with a 42-week course and ended with flying the North American T-28 Trojan. The VNAF pilots then went to Hurlburt Field at Eglin AFB, where they received flight instruction on the A-1. Training of these first VNAF Skyraider pilots was conducted by a lone U.S. Navy pilot, Lieutenant Ken Moranville, in April 1960 at NAS Corpus Christi. Lieutenant Moranville then proceeded to Tan Son Nhut, where he continued training the fledgling VNAF pilots. Initial USAF training of VNAF pilots was conducted by the 4440th Combat Crew Training Wing at Eglin AFB, Florida.

Many of the early missions in dual-control A-1Es were flown with U.S.

A 516th FS A-1H (139707) taxis back to its revetment at DaNang in 1966 with the wings folded. VNAF A-1s had the tailhook assembly removed, but kept the wing-folding mechanism. Many alert aircraft kept their wings folded until take-off to keep the sun from making the cockpit unbearable. (Tom Hansen)

WARBIRD**TECH**
SERIES

A VNAF crew chief guides a 518th FS A-1H (134621) out of its revetment at Bien Hoa in 1970, loaded with Mk. 82 LDGP bombs and the usual oil-soaked Mk. 8 drop tank. VNAF A-1s also had the nose flaps fixed in the open position for added cooling. (USAF)

Air Force advisors in the left seat and VNAF crews in the right seat. This met the Geneva Accords restrictions on combat intervention by a foreign national. In-country training of VNAF crews later was conducted by the Air Force 34th Tactical Group and Detachment Zulu of VA-152. Considered part of the OJT training program of VNAF pilots, the U.S. crews were also flying combat missions against Viet Cong targets in South Vietnam.

The VNAF was equipped with both single-seat A-1Hs and dual-control A-1Es and Gs. The VNAF 1st Fighter Squadron, equipped with AD-6 Skyraiders, began combat operations from Tan Son Nhut in May 1961. Their mission was counter-insurgency against the Viet Cong guerrillas and North Vietnamese Army troops that were operating in South Vietnam. VNAF A-1s were used to bomb the palace of President Diem during the November 1962 coup that overthrew the Diem government. Nguyen Ca Ky was commander of the VNAF at the time, and it is said that he gave the order to attack Diem's palace.

An A-1E (132503) from the 514th FS, 23 Tactical Wing, has a recently installed new rear canopy that was pulled from an AD-5W. A-1s, whether USAF or VNAF, always had a problem with spare parts. The 514th FS was based at DaNang in 1968. (Richard Kamm)

A 514th FS A-1H on the ramp at Tan Son Nhut in December 1970 carrying a pair of 750-pound M117 bombs, and six Mk. 82 500-pound bombs. The aircraft has obviously been repainted around the black-and-yellow checkered band, which indicates a squadron change. (Robert F. Dorr)

A trio of 23rd Tactical Wing A-1Hs rest on the ramp outside the covered revetments at Tan Son Nhut. USAF Red Horse personnel built a great many of these covered revetment when VC mortar attacks against the air bases began to increase in intensity. Note the variation in markings on the three aircraft, all from the 516th FS, right down to different prop tip markings. (Norman E. Taylor)

In May 1964, the United States transferred 50 A-1Es and 25 A-1Hs to the VNAF. By August 1964, the VNAF was considered a viable force in conducting combat operations against defended targets. Consequently, offensive operations against targets inside North Vietnam began shortly after the Tonkin Gulf Incident brought U.S. forces into the conflict. With U.S. Air Force and Navy aircraft winning air superiority over North Vietnam, the VNAF Skyraiders began ranging north of the DMZ, flying interdiction missions against the truck traffic that brought men and supplies into South Vietnam. The first such mission was flown by VNAF Skyraiders on March 1, 1965. Those missions ended when the Soviet Union installed radar-directed anti-aircraft weapons and surface-to-air missiles to defend the North.

A very interesting pair of photos of the same VNAF A-1H (139691), which crashed near An Khe in 1967. The A-1H was picked up by a U.S. Army CH-54 Skycrane and transported back to An Khe to be stripped and scrapped or taken to a repair facility. The aircraft has a different set of markings on each side—the new 514th FS marking on the left side, with the old style on the right side. (Larry McMillan)

As USAF phased A-1s out of service, the VNAF gladly put them in service. Most of the USAF A-1s were in far better condition than any VNAF aircraft. This A-1H (52-139770) retains its USAF-style serial. It also shows other USAF modifications, including the Yankee Extractor seat and the replacement solid wheels, as it taxis at Phu Cat in 1972. (Tom Brewer)

Vietnamese Air Force Skyraider operations continued over the South until the end of the war, even though President Nixon's Vietnamization program called for replacement of the A-1s by Northrop F-5 and Cessna A-37 jet aircraft. During the 1972 Easter Offensive, the North Vietnamese were equipped with Soviet shoulder-fired, heat-seeking SA-7 Strella missiles, which brought down a number of Allied aircraft, including a VNAF A-1 and three Air Force A-1s on May 1 and 2, 1972. A large number of A-1s were captured by the invading North Vietnamese troops as they took the country by force in 1975.

A VNAF 23rd TW A-1E returns to Bien Hoa in September 1972 following another mission against the NVA invasion troops that operated around An Loc. Several VNAF A-1s were shot down by SA-7 STELLA shoulder-fired, heat-seeking missiles during the early stages of the 1972 NVA Easter Offensive. (Robert F. Dorr)

During the fall of South Vietnam in 1975, several A-1s were ferried to Thailand by escaping VNAF pilots. Of those, four are known to have been brought back to the United States and put into restored, flying condition. The last word from the U.S. Air Force Museum is that one of the A-1Hs captured by the North Vietnamese in 1975 has been brought back and will be displayed at the museum in the future.

When the NVA launched the final offensive in March 1975, which resulted in the collapse of South Vietnam, a number of VNAF pilots escaped in anything that would fly, including several A-1s. This 23rd Tactical Wing A-1E (133919) was the last A-1 out of South Vietnam, landing at Utapao AB, Thailand, in May 1975. (Don Jay)

SIGNIFICANT DATES

1 MAY 1940
First flight of the Douglas SBD Dauntless.

30 JUNE 1941
Navy Dept. issues a contract for the Douglas XSB2D-1.

8 DECEMBER 1941
United States enters World War Two.

5 JUNE 1942
SBD Dauntless dive bombers distinguish themselves at Battle of Midway.

17 MARCH 1943
First XSB2D-1 is finished.

FALL 1943
Navy Dept. changes the basic requirements for dive and torpedo bombers.

15 FEBRUARY 1944
Rollout of the first BTD-1 Destroyer.

JULY 1944
Navy Dept. cancels the contract for the BTD-1 Destroyer.

JULY 1944
Douglas engineers make a formal proposal for the XBT2D-1 Dauntless II.

14 AUGUST 1944
Inspection and approval of the XBT2D-1 mockup.

MARCH 1945
Rollout of the XBT2D-1.

18 MARCH 1945
First flight of the XBT2D-1.

5 MAY 1945
Navy Dept. contract for 548 BT2D-1 Dauntless IIs.

14 AUGUST 1945
World War Two ends.

FEBRUARY 1946
BT2D-1 Dauntless II is renamed Skyraider.

APRIL 1946
Navy Department re-designates the BT2D-1 as the AD-1.

5 NOVEMBER 1946
Rollout of the AD-1 Skyraider.

6 DECEMBER 1946
First squadron operational in the AD (VA-19A).

APRIL 1947
AD Skyraider Carrier Qualification Tests conducted by VA-3B and VA-4B.

EARLY 1948
AD-2 production begins.

MAY 1948
AD-3 production begins.

25 JUNE 1950
Korean War breaks out.

3 JULY 1950
First AD strikes against North Korean targets by VA-55, *USS Valley Forge*.

17 AUGUST 1951
First flight of the AD-5.

NOVEMBER 1951
Royal Navy obtains 50 AEW-1s (AD-4W) under MDAP program.

21 MAY 1953
An AD-4B from VA-301 sets World Lift Record.

27 JULY 1953
Korean War ends.

JUNE 1954
Peak production of AD Skyraider at 59 per month.

23 FEBRUARY 1955
BuAer changes basic tactical color scheme from Navy Blue to Gull Grey and Gloss White.

SEPTEMBER 1955
Peak Navy operations with the AD at 29 squadrons.

18 FEBRUARY 1957
Last AD Skyraider rolls off the Douglas assembly line.

1959
France obtains 93 ADs under MDAP.

23 SEPTEMBER 1960
First AD-6s delivered to Vietnamese Air Force in Saigon.

4 NOVEMBER 1961
Operation FARM GATE begins USAF operations at Bien Hoa.

1962
Department of Defense redesignates all AD aircraft as A-1.

1 MAY 1964
First Air Force A-1Es delivered to FARM GATE detachment at Bein Hoa.

5 AUGUST 1964
Operation PIERCE ARROW, first Navy A-1 air strikes against North Vietnam.

5 AUGUST 1964
First U.S. Navy A-1 loss in Vietnam War.

1 MARCH 1965
Operation ROLLING THUNDER begins.

MAY 1965
First carriers on Dixie Station off South Vietnam.

20 JUNE 1965
First A-1 MiG kill in Vietnam by VA-25 pilots.

28 APRIL 1967
Douglas merges with McDonnell Aircraft Corp.

20 FEBRUARY 1968
Last Navy A-1 attack squadron combat launch by VA-25, *USS Coral Sea*.

10 APRIL 1968
Navy retires the A-1 attack plane at NAS Lemoore.

27 DECEMBER 1968
Last Navy A-1 combat launch (VAQ-33 EA-1F).

30 MARCH 1972
NVA launch Easter Offensive.

7 NOVEMBER 1972
Last Air Force A-1 combat mission in Vietnam War.

27 JANUARY 1973
Negotiated peace in Vietnam.

21 FEBRUARY 1973
Negotiated peace in Laos.

14 AUGUST 1973
Negotiated peace in Cambodia.

29 AND 30 APRIL 1975
South Vietnam falls.

MAY 1975
Last Vietnamese Air Force A-1s flee to Thailand after the fall of South Vietnam.